Being told to perse
entirely different thin
and encourages us all
seems overwhelming.

—Dan Seaborn
President and Founder, Winning At Home, Inc.

Mountains of Mercy is the inspiring story of a mother's irre-pressible hope in the face of relentless challenges. Lavone Genzink's story is told with a quiet grace and peace-filled con-fidence that demonstrates God's gifts of strength of mercy in our moments of greatest need. Over the course of her mar-riage, Lavone experienced the grief of losing a child, meet-ing the overwhelming needs of her seven children, who faced life-threatening health issues, and caring for her physically disabled husband. Even as trials crashed and surged like the pounding surf, Lavone's faith remained strong. *Mountains of Mercy* renews our faith in the truth that God's grace always meets us where our sufficiency fails.

—Shelly Beach
award-winning co-author of Love Letters from the Edge:
Meditations for Those Struggling with Brokenness,
Trauma, and the Pain of Life

Through life-threatening illnesses, one heart-breaking diagno-sis after another, and tragic loss—each in itself a trial of Job-like proportions—Lavone Genzink not only has a peace that passes all understanding but has the ability to share it with all those who cross her path. *Mountains of Mercy* is a truly inspiring story of absolute faith in the God who has promised never to give us more than we can bear, but who has also promised abundant blessing, regardless of our circumstances. That truth is woven throughout this remarkable story.

—Sharon K. Souza
author of The Color of Sorrow Isn't Blue

Show me someone who has a genuine walk with the Lord, and I'll show you someone who has suffered. And again, that proved to be true when I read this book. Von has been in my Bible study for years—in the front row, in fact—and I have watched her commitment and desire to know who her Savior is grow year after year through the study of God's Word. The fruit of God's Spirit shines through her face and in her actions even in the worst of times, which is proof that her relationship with the Lord is real and that suffering seems to be the cement that keeps it all together and keeps her faith strong. I love her and I love her book.

—**Lynelle Pierce**
author, singer, speaker

This is Lavone Genzink's remarkable true story of her family's almost unimaginable triumph of faith over failure, hope over hopelessness, and advantage over adversity. Thank God that so few of us have to endure such relentless tragedy to appreciate the blessings showered on us daily by the grace of God and the redemption given us by our Savior Jesus Christ.

—**Fred Feldman**
Holland, Michigan

A powerful and heartfelt story of a family's trials and tribulations: because this life trial is experienced by such a likeable and loving family, it transcends pain and loss and becomes inspirational.

—**Dr. Joshua A. Cebula**
Holland, Michigan

As a physician, I am always humbled by the stories of perseverance, fortitude, and faith in the patients and families I care for. I can honestly say that I knew that Jordan and his family were some of the most steadfast in their faith, despite the hurdles life gives them. However, I never fully understood their whole story until I had the great pleasure to read this novel.

Thank you for providing these stories. You can only imagine the support this will provide for others going through trials and tribulations. I am deeply humbled and grateful for being blessed with the opportunity to care for Jordan.

—**Julia Steinke, MD,**
Helen De Vos Children's Hospital,
Grand Rapids, Michigan

In thirty years of ministry I've never met a person who has found more persistent joy in the face of suffering than Von Genzink. Von is living confirmation that hope always has the last word when Christ journeys with us through suffering. As I read *Mountains of Mercy* I had renewed assurance that nothing can separate us from the love of God that is in Christ Jesus. I plan on keeping multiple copies on my shelf and sharing them with anyone who seeks to believe that God is capable of transforming suffering into an abundant life in Christ.

—**Rev. Keith Doornbos**
Pastor, Providence Church
Holland, Michigan

The title for this book, *Mountains of Mercy*, is well chosen. Vonnie Genzink and her family have had to climb mountains—steep, dangerous, discouraging, frightening mountains. Her ongoing faith makes sense only if the Bible makes sense. Otherwise, her insistence that there is a loving God makes no sense, that is, nonsense.

One of her quotes from the Bible is from the book of James, that we are to "count it all joy when we fall into various testings." Have you ever met someone who actually lives that invitation? Vonnie and her husband do. But the "happy spirit" she was born with can take her only so far. It is her "peace with God" that keeps her from "fighting with him." The author helpfully demonstrates that her "absolute confidence that God loves me" in no way keeps her from struggling to accept the plan He has for her. In the end, the highest mountain of all is God's loving presence.

—**Rev. Ren Broekhuizen,**
Retired Pastor, Ridge Point Community Church
Holland, Michigan

An honest and unfiltered story of the faithfulness of God through trials and crisis. *Mountains of Mercy* will have you singing and dancing, crying and laughing as it gives life to the hope and healing that is found in the resurrected Christ Jesus as we submit ourselves to his plans for our lives.

—**David Mosterd**
Chaplain and Director of Student Life
Holland Christian High School

MOUNTAINS
OF MERCY

MOUNTAINS OF MERCY

ONE FAMILY'S STORY OF HOPE IN CRISES

Lavone D. Genzink
with Latayne C. Scott

Dedication

I want to dedicate this book to my heavenly Father. I pray that all the glory goes to him. Without his unconditional love and sacrifice, I would not have the faith, grace, peace, and gift to live with him forever, and I want to glorify him with this book. All the strength and perseverance I have received is from him; no one can sustain death, illness, or trials without God carrying them through.

Acknowledgments

I want to thank Latayne for putting my memories and words into story form. Thank you for helping me tell my story so that others can find hope to go through trials of their own.

Thank you, Gary. Without you, this book would have only been a dream. Thanks to you and your support this dream has come true. Love you.

My mom is my rock, and without her I would not be the woman I am today. She, with her example of living with grace through experiencing trials of her own, helped me immensely. I appreciate her for her love, her wisdom, for allowing me to use her as a sounding board, and for lifting me up by being my prayer warrior. I could not have done it without you, Mom. Thank you for everything. Love you so much.

My husband and my children are my greatest blessings. They are the greatest gifts given to me. My world has been made complete with them in it. The Lord blessed me with children who through all our mountains learned what is right and wrong and lived a life with great maturity. They made decisions pleasing to Christ and put others first. They are humble, Christian young men and women, and no mother could be prouder. I love you all with all my heart. Thank you for being you.

Ron, I pray this book gracefully reflects what you have gone through and represents your humble and loving heart for the Lord. I hope that you are touched by all who read it. Thank you for your love. I love you.

Contents

Part One

SNAPSHOTS

1

Renovations

Does everyone have a defining moment in life, a snap-shot of a scene where something happens that seems to set the stage for all coming days?

Mine came the day my husband-to-be presented me with an early wedding gift. I already thought I'd won the lottery when this handsome, lanky, blue-eyed young man started talking about marriage. After all, he'd had girlfriends since kindergarten (some of whom he'd plied with gifts of jewelry filched from his mother's jewelry box).

He had chosen me, and now he had bought me a house. It was two months before he formally asked for my hand, and perhaps he was testing me. He couldn't wait to show me "our house." As we neared the turnoff on that bright May morning, he began rubbing a hand through his thick dark hair. As we rounded the last corner, I saw it—the two-story home in the distance.

"It has six acres with it," he said. I strained forward, looking.

"And it needs a little work," he added.

As we got closer, I saw what he meant. The front door was open at an angle, and goats were running in and out. The outbuildings leaned precariously. The grass was so tall you could hardly walk through it, and there were mysterious scurrying sounds beneath it if you stopped to listen. Bullet holes marked the siding of the house, and paint peeled off in ribbons.

The smell inside met us at the door: rotting food in the refrigerator, even an abandoned bowl of cereal and milk. Everything about this house was crazy. The water heater had been dragged into the kitchen, and a mattress lay beside it. Drug paraphernalia littered the floor.

"I really like the front screen door," I ventured. I squinted and thought to myself that its frilly decorations looked sort of Victorian.

"I heard it was built before the Chicago fire of 1893," Ron offered.

"We can fix it up!" I said.

Unfortunately, the house's only charm, the screen door, disappeared before we took possession. Almost all the rest of our dates, up until we were married on April 16, 1982, were spent at the house. Other people could socialize, we reasoned. We would get to know each other by renovating.

My first task was to use a push mower to try to clear a path around the house. I found the source of the scurrying sound—every few feet the blades would catch and then spit up a filleted dead mouse. And then there was the goat manure, knee-high in places. I learned to wield a shovel and not breathe at the same time.

I found the foundations for an old barn and silo. Broken dishes crunched underfoot. But there were loaded-down apple, pear and cherry trees, blackberry bushes, and grapevines too.

Ron began to tackle cleaning the metal siding, and I helped him with that. Friends and family came for a painting day, and at the end we fried hamburgers for them and surveyed our new, slate blue house.

The barn got a coat of red paint, and four new residents—four horses I learned to saddle and ride. Loved ones and neighbors continued to help us through the whole long process of restoring the house to its former glory. The inside had to be gutted—and revealed in its innards the bottles, yellowed newspapers, and even an old cane that had been stuffed in as insulation. With a new floor plan walls went up, new windows sparkled, and all the stripped trim and doors gleamed with new stain.

Little by little we were building our future. Our house was our life.

Those were good days. I remember kind neighbors who welcomed us with a potluck block party. Painting outside with my cousin Mary, watching *Little House on the Prairie* with an extension cord running out the window. Chasing after runaway horses that outsmarted the new electric fence. Dodging a hammer that escaped Ron's hand and whizzed just inches from my head. Was he trying to kill me before we even got married? I asked. Hardly, he answered. I had to stay healthy to bear those four children we would have, if God allowed.

Twelve, I said under my breath—twelve.

We talked and dreamed of the future, and our dreams came true. Our April wedding was yellow crinoline and parasols and mums and red roses and ivory and baby blue tuxes. We didn't serve alcohol for the sake of teetotaler in-laws and hired a mathematician, Barry Richardson, who did magic using mathematics to entertain our guests. In a borrowed pickup with a camper from my parents, we left for our two-week, cross-country honeymoon, to Florida, stopping where we wanted along the way.

But our home was calling us, and we came back earlier than we'd first planned. Plastic sheets hung on both sides of the living room to keep out the dust. Only the bedroom, bathroom, and kitchen (except for the cabinets) were finished. The upstairs was an echoing realm of possibilities. We repaired and added to the house in almost every spare moment when I wasn't working at a hair salon or Ron as a carpenter for a builder.

Almost every spare moment. I rode our horses, my hair streaming out behind me with the winds of freedom and hope. We ate TV dinners sitting in front of our little old black and white. We had a German shepherd puppy named Heidi who rode in the front seat of the car with us. We were gloriously happy.

In the middle of the room on the bare floor sat a table saw, and it stayed there for a long time. It was a symbol of what our lives were then, and of what they have become: a project constantly under construction, being built up as we grew, and constantly being renovated by the Lord.

2

A Surgery and a Birth

The eye doctors blamed the house. Ron had been having double vision and headaches, and he was just straining his eyes too much with all the construction work, they said. "Slow down," they said.

He didn't. Always determined, he just hammered away with one eye closed. Our home began to reflect our happiness with its order and beauty. And a little over a year after our wedding, I had good news.

I shared the news with Ron's father. He leaned against his trailer and asked, "Are you sure that's what you really want?"

I couldn't stop laughing. A pregnancy! What I had dreamed about since I was a little girl. I felt better than I'd ever felt in my life. It was as though everything in our life was hurtling toward a happily ever after.

Except that Ron's vision was getting more troublesome. And a hearing loss that had started after high school seemed to take on greater importance. The next doctor—an ear, nose and throat specialist—didn't think the house had caused anything and ordered a

CT scan. The next morning the ringing phone woke us up. It was a tumor, a golf-ball sized one, right in the middle of Ron's brain. Radiation, recommended one doctor. Do a biopsy first, advised another, at a nearby teaching hospital.

A biopsy it was. Friday the thirteenth of January, 1984, six weeks before my due date. Ron gave his consent to this date because he wasn't superstitious, and he wanted to get it over with.

There are things I regret about my life, and one of them is that I didn't linger in Ron's room with him before he went in. I wish I'd stayed there, hugging him like I wanted to. But my cousin Mary was waiting for me in the hallway, and I kissed him goodbye.

The biopsy was scheduled for, and lasted, over eight hours. I wondered how long a surgery would have lasted if this was only a biopsy. His incision would run, the doctor said, from the top of his head down to the nape of his neck in the back. When the procedure was done, the doctors had good news and bad news.

The good news was the type of tumor: a germinoma.

"It's probably been growing inside him since he was a little boy," the doctor said. It was cancer, but a slow-growing type that would respond well to radiation. Then came the bad news. Radiation, the doctor told us soberly, would destroy any chance of Ron and me having any more children.

The rest of Ron's recovery was rocky: more than a week in intensive care, the insertion of a shunt for drainage, and another week in the hospital. Ron's depth perception and spirits were poor, and he still had double vision. Worst of all, the procedure had nicked a nerve, affecting his balance, which he has not regained to this day.

His radiation treatments began in February, five days a week. Again, our friends and family came to our aid and helped with transportation for him and other necessities. Now four weeks away from delivery, I was anticipating a Leap Year baby. We took Lamaze classes and worked as a team, preparing for our big day.

Because Ron couldn't work, he became anxious about making sure the house was ready. He was only twenty-four years old, yet he walked with a cane and was losing his hair because of his treatments. Still, he needed to contribute to our home. We'd prepared a small portion off the living room as a nursery. Ron couldn't see to drive nails, but he was determined to work. He drilled a hole in a board, and whenever he needed to put finishing nails into the baseboards he just inserted a nail in the hole, used it for positioning, and hammered away.

On February 28 our nine-and-a-half pound baby boy, Joshua Jay Genzink, met the world. A team of student nurses who'd never witnessed a birth stood breathlessly outside the room.

"Can we watch?" one of them asked.

"Sure!" I agreed, between gasps.

Ron sat on a stool near me, his red stocking cap covering his bare head, his beard thinning, looking frail and tired. But Joshua gave his father renewed strength. I think he was glad to have the focus off himself, and God gave him great joy. When God gives us a closed door, he always blesses us with an open window. And ours was filled with light!

Just after Joshua was baptized in March, we learned more wonderful news.

"The tumor is gone," the doctor said. We felt as though we'd been given two gifts, two lives, and true happiness.

From the time Ron was diagnosed I had been so joyful that people warned me about being unrealistic. For example, when Ron's procedure started early in the morning, we knew it would take about eight hours. (Imagine a biopsy taking all day—we wouldn't have

known what to do with a full-blown surgery.) The CT
scan hadn't given them much information, so the team
made an incision from the top of his head to the nape of
his neck. The procedure went slowly, and a nurse came
out periodically to report progress. During that biopsy
I sat in the waiting room with Ron's parents and other
family members. Looking back, perhaps I seemed too
casual, too cheerful in the midst of his other relatives
who were deeply concerned about a bad outcome to the
surgery. I don't know how to look at that, even now—
that's just the way I am. I am positive. I feel God gave me
the gift of acceptance.

And right then I felt I needed to be positive. I was
pregnant, and I needed my husband. I was going to fight
to keep him for as long as I could. I wouldn't give up. It
seemed then, as it seems now, only logical to look for the
best. Why worry about what is going to happen if you
don't know what it will be?

I have struggled with how people perceive me when
I am at peace with God and joyful even in the midst
of difficult situations. I know others must see this as
some kind of irrational hilarity, laughing when things
seem grim; they probably wonder how someone could
realistically look at a situation and feel such joy. But, like
the woman in Proverbs 31, I laugh at the future.

He will give you, too, the strength and grace to face
whatever it is, whenever it comes. And coming days
would test the strength of that conviction.

3

GRACE SUFFICIENT

I remember the first time I met Ron. It was like one of those improbable movie plots, with mistaken identities and innocent little intrigues designed to get to know someone.

He was 6'2" and lanky, jaw-dropping handsome, with thick dark hair and startling blue eyes. Even his teeth were beautiful, I thought, the first time I saw him, sitting in a booth at a restaurant called The Salad Bowl with two of his cousins. I'd just returned from a ski trip with a girlfriend, and we were ready for another adventure.

"Aren't you Rick Genzink?" I innocently asked Ron's cousin, and with that introduction we invited the three young men to come and sit with us. Both Rick and Steve Genzink were single, but as the conversation continued my heart sank. Ron showed me the photograph of his girlfriend, Patty. He had a diamond ring on layaway. I turned my attention to Rick, and as we parted company Rick expressed that we'd see each other again.

That winter, though, I couldn't stop thinking about Ron. And apparently, Ron had thought about girls, too.

He was quiet, kind-natured and well spoken. Only an average student in school, he was very popular and active on the soccer team. Much of his free time was spent with friends or riding his motorcycle. He had begun drinking and smoking in his mid teens and worked at a local car wash. He was like a sweet James Dean with a mullet.

His college plan was to get a degree in architectural drafting. But when he took a summer job as a carpenter with a friend named Jack DeFrell, all of that changed. Woodworking became a passion for Ron, and he was gifted with the ability, people said, to do anything with a piece of wood. Wood was more than a raw material for him; it was canvas and paint in the hands of an artist.

So when I met Ron his life seemed set, going in a direction that did not include me. I did see his cousin Rick again at a skating rink, and Ron too. With mutual friends we all "hung out" at local eateries.

November, December and January crawled by, in the frigid air of Michigan. I was watching Ron, and he was watching me. What I didn't know on that fateful Saturday in February of 1979 is that Ron had broken up with his girlfriend the night before. Ron and I and a group of friends went to the same pizza restaurant where I'd first met him. After the meal, as we lingered before venturing out into the stinging-cold air outside, Ron hesitated. He drew me close to him and with one tender, unforgettable kiss ambushed my heart. I was in love with him. But he said he'd fallen in love with me already.

"I can tell you the exact moment," he said. "It was when I was kneeling next to you at the skating rink, tying your skates for you. That's when I knew."

We began dating, and spring came, and then summer.

But by July I was having second thoughts. Having just turned twenty, I broke up with Ron—and began dating other guys, among them another by the name of Ron.

One week the "other" Ron and a third young man I had also been dating both sent me red roses. I felt like Cinderella at the ball, with two Prince Charmings wanting to dance with me.

Soon, though, the field narrowed back down to two, Ron and Ron. I struggled with the decision; even at the time I realized I was making a decision not just about boyfriends but about my future husband. Both young men were respectful, and I enjoyed spending time with them. (And there were other factors: one was a better kisser, the other a better conversationalist.)

The significance of such decisions has stayed with me. Ron had chosen me and had even chosen to break off his engagement to another young woman in order to pursue me. And I, after much soul-searching, chose him, knowing that others were interested in me. For our thirty years of marriage we have had the assurance that neither of us had just "settled" for the other. We were each other's first choice, chosen from among alternatives.

We talked a lot about that; promises are easily given when everything is pleasant and the future looks bright. We said the words "for better or for worse," . . . and our circumstances have in many ways gotten consistently and persistently worse! We said we wanted to marry for richer or for poorer, and though we have never been in want for the things we needed, our married life never materialized into the upward mobility of finances I think we naturally expected. And, of course, the phrase "in sickness and in health" was so easy to roll off the tongue when we both were young and vigorous and unafraid.

While we were dating we often went north for the weekend to Silver Lake. Ron's parents had a vacation home there, and we loved the swimming and boating. Also in the area were sand dunes to climb or—in Ron's case—to race cars over. Nearby was a youth camp run by a local church.

Just as important to me, looking back now, is a tradition we began on our visits. There was a special tree with a large rock near it, and each time we went Ron and I would take photos of each other at that spot. Those early photos were of two carefree young people, with stars in their eyes and no fear of the future. (I wouldn't have had it any other way, even though those stars have dimmed and our lives together have brought much to be feared.)

But within months the photographs of us in other places would have looked very different. First, of course, would be pictures of us working on the house. Later would be wedding portraits. Then one would show me pregnant, another with a tiny baby in my arms. Ron, though, would have transformed from an active and kinetic young man into a husband and father stripped to the core of his capabilities by cancer, surgery, and radiation.

Perhaps it's irrelevant, but I sometimes wonder what I would have told myself if I could have gone back in time to my twenties, when Ron's health problems began. We were just married, madly in love, and all that passion and hope were exemplified in the new life that was growing inside me. We were working daily on our house, and on our marriage. Our future wasn't even a future; it was just a short time, literally just days, of present. And then everything changed.

"Why us?" I asked at the time. I had married strong, athletic Ron for many reasons, but among them was my desire to have a protector. The irony was that suddenly, hardly out of my teens and heavily encumbered by pregnancy, I became his.

Once I had struggled to keep up with his long-legged stride; then he was the one who began to struggle to walk at all. The changes happened so imperceptibly I can hardly remember the progression. But I can tell you that we have arrived at an outcome of which I could never have dreamed.

From the beginning, Ron has had a very relaxed view of life. *Que será, será*—whatever will be, will be, has always been his philosophy. When we received the first diagnosis of cancer, I was devastated, but he never wavered in his faith.

"Everything will turn out all right," he told me, over and over. Literally and figuratively, he just sat back and waited to see how that "all right" would play out. In his weakened state he slept a lot, and both his memory and thinking processes seemed to slow down. Meanwhile, as he dozed, I was operating on overdrive.

We both breathed a sigh of relief when we learned that there were treatments available for his tumor. It wasn't just that there was a solution; it was the playing out of the truth of 2 Corinthians 12:9:

My grace is sufficient for you, for my power is made perfect in weakness. Therefore I will boast all the more gladly about my weaknesses, so that Christ's power may rest on me.

God's grace was sufficient for me. If, as that passage says, God's power is made perfect in weakness, then I was the perfect object of that grace, because I was very, very weak. But again and again God's power was strong. That grace, that unearned gift, kept me hopeful and optimistic. Somehow I was able to put myself aside and put God first, even while others continued to say I wasn't being realistic about the challenges we were facing.

"After all, this is brain cancer," people reminded us.

And they were right—no amount of positive thinking could change the circumstances. But God would help us *in* the circumstances.

There is a truth that has allowed us both to ride above such changes. Our circumstances are testimony to the truth that life can go from seemingly secure to situations that feel completely unanchored and adrift. But Isaiah 26:3 has not only kept us steady but has defined a path for us:

You will keep in perfect peace those whose minds are steadfast because they trust in you.

We will remain in peace as long as we trust Him, but if our minds aren't fully set on Him we cheat ourselves because we won't feel all the peace we could receive.

4

STRAIGHT PATHS

In some ways I believe that everything that happened to me before I met Ron prepared me for life with the challenges we have faced together. And I've been surprising people ever since my birth. I was born at a time when fathers waited outside while their wives delivered the babies. The nurse covered me up and took me to my father with instructions not to tell him anything, because my mother wanted to break the news to him.

"Oh no! What's wrong?" My father's voice trembled.

The news, contrary to his expectations but to his relief, was that he had a daughter. I remained without a name for three days because my parents had been so convinced they were having a boy; it wasn't until they together enjoyed a television show with an actress named Lavone that they settled on that for a first name.

Within the first two months of my life, though, I began to run high fevers. The doctors' subsequent predictions that I would be susceptible to every passing illness came true; before I started school I was hospitalized for pneumonia so many times my parents lost count.

My tonsils were removed in an attempt to boost my resistance, and this provided some respite, but when I began school I succumbed to chicken pox, measles, mumps, strep throat and other illnesses.

The antibiotics made my face swell up as large as a balloon. Though my parents never complained, I know this had to have been a tremendous financial burden on them. By the time I was six my exasperated parents took me to an allergy doctor, who found that I was allergic to both dust and mold.

As has happened so many times later in my life, people believed that this would be a final solution to my health problems, that a door would close on that and I would be healthy. But going for the allergy shots became a weekly ritual for my mother and me that stretched on for ten years.

Growing up in Zeeland, Michigan, in the 1960s was nonetheless a wonderful childhood. One house we lived in was so close to the railroad tracks that the dishes rattled in the cupboard every time the train passed by. When I was young my dad was the manager of a five and dime store and my mother a homemaker. The dynamics of the family changed a bit when I was three and my brother Daniel was born.

I was a tomboy with the neighborhood boys, riding bikes with them, playing cops and robbers and war with GI Joe dolls, and racing Matchbox cars through roads made of clothespins. My dad taught me car repair, and one of my favorite places was under the car with him. He taught my brother and me to hunt, shoot a rifle, ride motorcycles and water ski. When camping he let us pick mushrooms and joked with us that we would know they were poisonous if we didn't wake up the next morning. He made us a tree house and a zip line and a go-cart that, as I look back on it, probably endangered all our lives. But we loved it.

On the other hand, that was also a time of girly birthday parties, Girl Scout Brownie activities and working for merit badges, selling cookies, of day camps and crafts, marching in parades and riding on floats. Like any little girl in the sixties, I played with Barbie dolls and with neighborhood girls put on shows where I got to sing and entertain.

After my weekly bath my mom would curl my long hair around her finger and then secure it with bobby pins. People said I looked like Shirley Temple, something I've seen reflected in the dimples and curly hair of some of our own children.

But even in that happy childhood a certain fear began to grow in my heart. I wasn't able to go anywhere overnight without trying to pack every doll and other beloved toy to take with me. I was afraid of losing it all if it weren't with me. Even worse, I hated it when my parents went out at night and left my brothers and me with a babysitter. I was always afraid they wouldn't come back. The fear was even stronger when they were gone on overnight trips. I know that other people had such fears when they were children, but my fear was acute; unfortunately, in the case of my father, it was a fear that would come to be a reality.

Actually, my parents should have been much more worried about me than I was about them! Once I left a car door partially open, and as my mom began driving her purse, which had been wedged between me and the door, fell out. I was hanging out of the car trying to catch the contents of her purse when the car following ours careened to a stop at about the same time my mom noticed my predicament.

Another time in kindergarten I impulsively decided to walk to a new friend's house after school. From there, I called my mother to tell her where I was.

"You come right home!" she said.

But my new friend didn't know the way to my house and wouldn't come with me, and I ended up wandering on foot all the way across our little town. At first I didn't see any buildings I recognized. Finally, footsore and discouraged, I noticed a familiar storefront and found myself at my dad's workplace, knocking politely on the door.

Although my mom was both furious and relieved when he called her, my dad was proud of me.

"If you could find your way here, you can handle anything in life," he said proudly.

From my earliest memory, Proverbs 3:5–6 has been important to me, and it certainly proved itself to me that day:

Trust in the LORD with all your heart and lean not on your own understanding. In all your ways acknowledge him and he will make your paths straight.

I knew even then that God's making my paths straight involved more than finding my way home when I was lost. I have found that trusting the Lord is best because He has my life all worked out. He knows all the paths. I can't see the whole picture, and I don't know His reasons for the trials and dead-end paths and detours He has allowed me to follow, but I do know that He is in control, that He's mine, and that He will lead me in the direction I need to go.

I was brought up knowing Jesus and was convinced that He had made me and loved me. We prayed at meals and always before bed, reciting, "Now I lay me down to sleep . . ." I never doubted that I could go to God for anything.

My parents took us to Reformed churches, where I learned the Lord's Prayer and the 23rd psalm and the Heidelberg Catechism. I learned the simple children's songs about Jesus loving me; about His loving all children of all races, red and yellow, black and white; and about the

B-I-B-L-E. I loved Kate Smith's "Ten Thousand Angels" and the Bible verses and all my teachers.

Our family attended a church where my father was a deacon; the church life was part of us, and we were part of it. We attended Sunday school, and I helped with the nursery. In the summer I went to a Baptist church's vacation Bible school and learned about how we should march onward as Christian soldiers.

It was glorious.

But one place where I didn't exactly shine was in school. Even in the early grades I came to conclude that school was not my friend. The smell of chalk dust struck me dumb. I was shy and quiet and not very smart.

My second-grade teacher, Mrs. Hoffman, sent me out in the hall a lot because I was always talking in class. My third-grade teacher resorted to writing my name on the blackboard to try to settle me down. And my name was up there a lot.

A school play in the sixth grade brought a new challenge into our lives. My mother, the school secretary, stood looking at me from a distance and for the first time noticed I was standing crooked. More trips to new doctors, along with X-rays, resulted in a diagnosis of scoliosis, or curvature of the spine. I wore a lift in my right shoe, and most embarrassing of all for an adolescent, I had to wear a back brace that I hid under baggy clothes all through high school.

But the roomy blouses didn't fool anyone. I was underdeveloped in all the places I wanted to be developed, a literal ninety-pound weakling. I was the object of perennial teasing and sometimes cruel jokes. When classmates strung toilet paper all over the trees in our front yard, it wasn't because I was popular.

I tried to hide wherever I went but was completely unaware of many of the things that must have isolated me from others. For instance, it never occurred to me to shave my legs or wear makeup until I was a junior in high school.

Growing up in a neighborhood full of younger children, I found great satisfaction in babysitting. My mom instructed me to leave a house cleaner than I found it—and I did, even when watching five little children at the going rate of fifty cents an hour. I dreamed of the day I would have a dozen children of my own. This was good practice, I thought to myself. All I had to do was find a husband who would go along with my plan.

Later on I found the same kind of satisfaction in service at a local nursing home where I began working when I was sixteen. I saw the loneliness of my own heart mirrored in those of people who had come to the end of their lives, often never visited by their own families. Of course, starting out on the bottom rung of employment there, I was the one to feed them, brush their teeth, give baths, change their diapers, and even clean their bottoms.

To my surprise this brought me great joy and satisfaction. I learned to love these fragile people and enjoyed taking them for walks. We welcomed some of them into our home for holidays. And, before long, at the age of seventeen, I was promoted to manager of one floor of the facility.

My life was a busy one—I attended high school in the mornings and a cosmetology school in the early afternoons before working some days at the nursing home and others at my parents' business that designed machinery for the plastics industry. (Of course I really wanted to be in the shop, welding and getting dirty, but I worked in the office.) With my dad cosigning the loan, I bought a brand new black Buick Regal and loved the freedom it gave me.

My life was centered around the Lord, my work with the elderly, training for a beloved career making people more beautiful, and the struggle to get through high school. But along the way I had learned much about serving people, about illness and dashed hopes and dreams.

Until I was out of high school I didn't date much. Imagine, then, my delight when the handsomest man I'd ever seen asked me to marry him. And how little I realized at the time how my life *before* Ron had prepared me for my life *with* Ron.

5

TRUST ON A ROLLERCOASTER

If I could be immortalized in a snapshot of a single moment of my life, a time when I was happiest, it would have to have been in a grocery store. Although this scenario happened many times, it remains the essence of satisfaction to me—to have Ron with me, the two of us pushing two grocery carts with our tribe of little children in tow. Oh, the looks we would get!

But that snapshot of our life would show what training children in the Lord can produce: respectful, joyful, unique individuals who were growing up—indeed, have now grown up—to honor us as parents and to be hard workers in all they do.

When our first child, Joshua, was born, it seemed as though God was communicating something to us. My pregnancy was unexpected and so early in our marriage that friends and family alike questioned the timing. But Joshua's birth on February 28, 1984, just weeks after Ron's diagnosis with a brain tumor, made it seem as though God was comforting us after all the sadness and trauma of the cancer. In fact, we believe this roly-poly little baby gave Ron renewed strength and helped us all take the unwelcome focus off him.

Joshua was baptized on March 18, and shortly thereafter a doctor gave us good news: the radiation on Ron had been successful. Just as they'd suspected, the type of cancer (which usually occurs in children) was slow growing and had responded well to radiation treatment.

And now Ron's brain tumor was completely gone! A double blessing! But with the good news came a sobering prediction. "The radiation treatment probably rendered Ron sterile," a doctor said gravely. As we looked at our precious new baby, it was with the understanding that he might be our only child. Not only that, but Ron's condition after the cancer treatment had left him weak, unable to keep his balance or see well, with hearing loss, and now unable to keep a job.

Why did all of this happen? To this day I'm not sure. I know that God knows and that He has a plan that we do not understand. We were obedient, kept faith and hope, and clung to God to get us through. One verse that was important to us was Jeremiah 29:11, which says

"For I know the plans I have for you," declares the Lord, "plans to prosper you and not to harm you, plans to give you hope and a future."

I relied on God and his plans for my life then, as I do now. Contrary to what our culture teaches, I do that *not* by "taking charge of my life" but by letting God handle it. I don't seek direction by digging into a computer for information to educate myself. I wait, pray, and hope for strength and perseverance to see and accept God's plan for me.

With that attitude, accepting that God had already given us double blessings so early in our marriage, imagine our delight when we found that another baby was on the way. To be honest, though others might have said "Oops!" our reaction was "Whee!" The doctors had been wrong!

On July 6, 1985, our Misty was born. She was a beautiful child, with dark hair and gorgeous dimples. We felt that our hope and faith had been vindicated. Actually, we named our new daughter Melista Dee. Her middle name was after my father, Dee. And just as we had seen a connection between the joy that Joshua had brought in the midst of Ron's cancer, we soon saw a connection between Melista Dee and her namesake. When she was just fifteen months old I received a phone call that devastated my world.

"Vonnie, I need to get ahold of Mom." My brother Daniel's voice was strange and strained on the telephone. I told him where to find her, and he choked up.

"It's Dad—he's dead."

"*What? How?*" I could barely get the words out. I knew Dad had left early in the morning to go deer hunting up north. But Daniel told me that en route he'd suffered a massive heart attack and died instantly. His car had drifted into oncoming traffic and hit a semi head-on.

It seemed so unfair. He was only fifty-four years old, had been married to Mom for only twenty-seven years. And now the man who'd taught me more life skills than I'd ever be able to thank him for was gone. All my childhood fears of my parents leaving and not coming back had come together in a terrifying and final reality. I hadn't lost possessions; I had lost something far more precious.

I collapsed in shock. Although no one else knew it, I had another life growing within me, and I began bleeding and nearly lost that baby.

How do you maintain faith when it seems that life is moving one step forward and two steps back? How do you trust God while on a rollercoaster?

Having children helped rather than hindered me spiritually. I had a firm foundation of assurance that God had kind intentions toward me. In Jeremiah 29:11–13, after the assurance that God knows His plans for us, we're promised:

> Then you will call on me and come and pray to me, and I will listen to you. You will seek me and find me when you seek me with all your heart.

I was indeed seeking Him with all my heart, and therefore I had no reason to doubt His motives or any outcomes they might bring in my life. In that stage of life, and indeed in all my life, I've gotten through these trials by not thinking about every detail and outcome. For me, it's better to just stay busy and active and positive and not get myself worked up with worry. My children were a great distraction, helping me to go on and keep busy. And I always remembered: where God closes a door, there is always an open window. I kept my eyes alert for those windows.

Our newest girl, born five months after my father's devastating death, we named Deidre, after a character in one of my favorite soap operas. But of course we called her DeeDee, after my dad, Dee D. Allen. This eight-pound blonde girl was strong from conception—a child who did somersaults in utero and lifted her head to look around at the world the day she was born, her clear blue eyes surveying her territory and yearning to bounce into it.

Like Isaac's welcoming of Rebekah after the death of his beloved mother, this energetic child brought comfort and peace to our household. Though it might have seemed like pandemonium to others outside our home with three young children and a disabled husband, to me it was the fulfillment of my lifelong dreams.

6

LIVING THE DREAM

My dream of having a large family started, I think, when Mom, Dad, and my brother Daniel and I would travel in the summer to visit Uncle Gerald and Aunt Theresa in nearby Vriesland, Michigan. They had two children the same ages as Daniel and me, and four others as well.

They lived in a large farmhouse at the end of a long gravel road, in the middle of wide open fields. There were so many places to play—a barn, a playhouse, and a tall bag swing that made thrilling arcs through the fresh country air. There were animals, too—but best of all were all the other children. Everything was more fun with more people.

I carried that fond memory with me, and as newlyweds Ron and I often talked about our dreams of a big family. "I'm living the dream," I'd tell him. "A house out in the country with a place for all my kids and animals, barefoot and pregnant." And I wouldn't have been joking very much.

DeeDee, our third child, was just an infant when, in December 1988, Ron became ill with pneumonia.

It seemed he couldn't get over it, and a doctor's examination brought some bad news: there was a lump on his throat that didn't look good.

"It's thyroid cancer," said a doctor after the biopsy. This would mean at the least that he would have to take thyroid medication for the rest of his life. After his thyroid was surgically removed, another biopsy revealed that the cancer hadn't been contained there. It was in his lymph nodes as well. The treatment for this was the administering of radioactive iodine.

"This man came toward me wearing a big radiation jacket and long gloves that reached to his elbows. He had a metal cup with a metal straw, and I had to drink from it," Ron says. "I felt like I was in some horror movie."

Some felt certain that this kind of radiation would prevent us from having any more children, but I found to my joy that I was expecting again. We felt the disapproval of some people, but never more acutely than when they passed along their opinions through our children. Someone actually asked our four-year-old son, "Why are your parents going to have another baby when your daddy could die any day now, since he's had two kinds of cancer?"

Of course this hurt us, but it hurt little Joshua the most, filling him with fear. Such thoughts had never entered our mind.

"God has healed your Daddy twice from cancer," we told him. "Why would we have any doubts about Him taking care of us, especially when He is blessing us with a new baby?"

People made snide remarks like, "Can I help you learn more about birth control?" Others were more intrusive: "How are you going to afford all those children?" "Do you really think you can send all of them to a Christian school?"

Of course the effect of such comments wasn't that we allowed others to make our decisions about our family size. It just meant that each time I became pregnant I waited longer to tell anyone outside the family.

To be honest, Ron and I have been comforted and affirmed by the fact that, in spite of his cancer and physical limitations, he has been able to father children. For my part, I can really identify with the women in the Bible who yearned and prayed for children. For women like us, having children is a soul-deep need, not just a whim.

Ron and I believed and clung to what the Bible says about children, and we have made a conscious decision to let the Bible's point of view about them be our point of view. Psalm 127:3–5 states that children are a heritage from the Lord, offspring a reward from Him. "Like arrows in the hands of a warrior are children born in one's youth," the Bible says, and we are so grateful for each one. We rejoice that our "quiver is full" and that we are blessed by having a large family.

And thus we welcomed our second son, Jordan, on August 2, 1989. Blond hair, blue eyes, seven pounds, fifteen ounces. Beautiful. My labor with him took all of fifteen minutes! We who should have been childless now had two boys and two girls. Four children! Who would have believed it? We were blessed, content, satisfied. We weren't rich, but we had a million-dollar family!

And we were busy! Our household was filled with joy, laughter and activity. By the time the holiday season of that winter approached, we would be praying for patience and endurance. And God, who gives and takes away, whose name is blessed forever, answered that prayer in ways we would never have expected.

7

"YOU FOOL!"

I knew from the earliest hours of Friday, November 17, 1989, that something bad was going to happen that day. This was the day that our oldest son, Joshua, was to have his first formal event in his kindergarten class, a Thanksgiving program for the school. Maybe it was just parent jitters. At five and a half, Josh was our first child in school, so emotions ran high for the whole family. Some of our initial fears had been groundless; our shy firstborn had acclimated well to school.

The day had started out as just another ordinary Michigan autumn day. The weather was cold and had that taste of invisible coming snow on it. Amidst the routine clamor of a household of toddlers, I got all the children up, dressed and fed. Our oldest, Joshua, was five, Misty four and Deedee two, and then there was our infant, Jordan.

Joshua loved being with people. From the time he was a toddler he would go with Ron to "coffee with the guys" on Saturday morning, where Joshua drank coffee-flavored milk in a mug and acted like a little man.

He loved being the center of attention there, in church, or wherever else he was.

He was a protector for his sister Misty, just sixteen months younger, and would call her "pretty girl." Now he'd made the big transition and been in kindergarten for a little over two months. On that cold November day it was time to practice for the Thanksgiving program that he and his classmates had so long prepared. He had approved of the new blue sweater, khaki pants, and gray shoes I'd bought him to wear that evening. But first there was a dress rehearsal. After leaving him at the practice I had that funny feeling again, as though something bad were going to happen.

Hearing shrill children's voices from outside, I ran to the window in alarm to see Misty and Deedee playing outside on the trampoline, an early Christmas gift from Ron and me. Was someone hurt? But all the squeals were of delight. I should stop worrying, I told myself, yet I couldn't seem to shake that terrible foreboding. I kept reassuring myself that everything was fine, and so I kept myself busy with laundry, housework and playing with the children.

Throughout the afternoon I thought about how blessed we were. The children gave me great fulfillment, and I was also leading a "Coffee Break" Bible study at church. Though Ron's health had leveled out, he was still unable to work; still, he didn't seem anxious about anything. We had discovered that little Misty had some substantial hearing problems, and she was being fitted for hearing aids. But other than those issues our lives seemed stable and manageable—even more, enjoyable.

I picked up Josh later that afternoon and brought him back home. We had dinner and then got dressed and ready to go to the program. I was still nursing and a little nervous about how Jordan would take a bottle. Maybe that was the dread feeling, I thought. I didn't want our babysitter to be overwhelmed by keeping up with three children ages four and under.

"I'll handle it," she assured us. "Go have a good time!"

The program was to begin at 7:00 p.m., but we needed to be there early so we could drop off Josh with his classmates to get lined up. There were parents and children everywhere. Every room in the basement was filled with the voices of excited children. Parents swabbed at little faces, tucked errant hairs back into place, and tugged at their children's clothes. Their teachers looked tired and anxious. Everyone wanted it to go smoothly.

I was holding Josh's hand as we went down the stairs to find his class. He was quiet and shy but didn't seem to mind when I dropped him off to join the other students. Even after I left him I went back at least three times to check on him, not letting him see me doing so. I was hoping it would ease the awful feeling I had, but it stuck with me.

The program was titled "Praise and Thanksgiving," and the principal welcomed everyone and then read Psalm 135, a passage of praise to God. It speaks of God's power, of his control over everything that happens to us. Even now I can look back at that Scripture and feel the reassurance it gave, assurance I didn't know I would need so much and so soon.

The students filed in and then sang. I was so proud of my little tow-headed son. Even from the distance I could see the dimple in his right cheek.

"He's the cutest one up there," Ron whispered. Taller than anyone else in his class, he was clearly visible amid the crush of students, high on the top row of the stage.

I remember that Josh was yawning as he sang. It was a late night with a lot of excitement for that little guy. As the kindergarten students were filing out, all the parents sat there waiting patiently, but Ron and I stood and waved to Joshua, trying to express how proud of him we were. Everyone looked at us as though we were crazy, but we didn't care. We found out later when we watched the video that Josh was waving to everyone, too, as he walked out of the church. He clutched like a treasure a roll of candy his teacher had given him.

It was a cold night and had begun to snow while we were in the program; when it was over the flakes were thick and heavy, turning into slush. We had an older red station wagon that we loved. Ron, Josh and I hopped into the front bench seat. We had made plans to go to a local restaurant for coffee and dessert with my mom and some friends who had a daughter, Amber, who was Josh's age.

I still had that uneasy feeling in the pit of my stomach and used the pay phone at the restaurant to call home a couple of times to make sure all the children were okay, still worried about three-month old Jordan. The sitter reassured me that everything was fine, and all the children were in bed.

At about 10:00 we decided it was time to go home. Amber and Joshua had secretly been making plans for a sleepover. When he asked, I told him no, and Don and Nancy agreed. Looking back, how I wish I'd said yes. Joshua hugged his grandmother. "I'm so proud of you!" she said over and over, watching his cute little behind walk away as we got into the car, our feet slipping in the snow. The flakes continued, slopping on the windshield in the dark. The ground and road were covered with icy moisture.

We were just one mile from home when it happened. Some people talk about sudden tragedies in their lives occurring in slow motion. But what we saw unfolding before us seemed to happen very much in real time.

We had just passed the corner of 142nd Street in East Saugatuck, heading south, when in the distance a northbound car began to lose control. We could see its lights, swerving back and forth in sickening curves, and as it neared us I could see it was a very large car. There was nothing we could do. It was implacable and determined. I had just given Joshua one of his candy prizes and was whispering to him, "I am so proud of you for your singing."

Ron's voice beside us was bitter and urgent. His eyes were on the disaster playing out before us. He spoke to the unseen driver: "You fool!" The car turned in front of us, and we hit it broadside on its passenger side with the shrieking sounds of metal meeting metal.

"You fool!" Then the car skidded and hit us on the driver's side. Ron slid underneath the steering wheel, and his lanky body was crumpled into the accelerator area, his back resting against the front of the seat. The first thing Ron remembers was Joshua's voice. "Mommy, it hurts."

"At least we're all still alive," Ron said. He tried to turn to reassure Joshua. I'm not sure what happened next because I blacked out. After I came to I grabbed Joshua and put him on my lap. I had no idea that both of my legs were injured. I never felt a thing as I held my son tightly in my arms. Something was very, very wrong with him.

Then there were voices around us, and the rhythmic strobe of emergency lights: "Were you wearing your seat belts?" It was a firefighter. I didn't understand why he was asking. We had been too excited about our evening, too happy to notice.

Later I learned that our car had stopped right in front of a house. A woman ran out to the car and stayed with me, talking and holding my hand, I was told. I don't remember any of that. But I do remember Joshua crying out in pain and arching his back and shaking his head, actions I later learned were signs of a head injury.

Another firefighter came and peered anxiously through the window.

"It's me, Cal Haverdink," he said.

"Oh, we have a Cal Haverdink at our church," Ron murmured.

"Ron, it's me."

I didn't know what to do; I was as disoriented as Ron. I knew Joshua was badly hurt. I remember hugging him, and he not saying a word. I thought of my father's recent death from a heart attack. I held my son close and whispered to him through my tears.

"Honey, you may go and be with Jesus and Grandpa Allen," I told him. I felt the warmth of his body, smelled the candy on his breath. "We will be okay. It's okay if you go." Then a firefighter took him from my arms, and I never saw him alive again.

8

BROKEN PEOPLE

Meanwhile, still inside our wrecked car, I was in and out of consciousness. One indelible memory was of emergency personnel cutting Ron out of the wreckage, extracting him with the "jaws of life." Like a horrible shower of deadly snowflakes, glass exploded all around us.

My visual memories of my own extraction are much less vivid. But when I was taken from the car the feeling apparently returned to my legs, and the pain was excruciating. I remember screaming. Then someone was putting some strange, inflatable pants on me.

The two ambulances that arrived first took Josh and the other driver, speeding away to the hospital. Until another ambulance arrived, they put me into the back of a pickup truck. The next thing that I remember is being in the emergency room.

"There's blood running into my eye," I told a nurse.

"It's from your broken nose," she said gently. Apparently the cold had frozen it before, and in the warmth of the hospital it began to drip. "Don't worry, I'll clean it up," she assured me.

All around me people were hurriedly cutting my overcoat and my other clothes away from my body. I was calm. Inexplicably, I had no pain. People ran in with monitors, with IV fluids, with cloths and blankets and bandages.

I looked beyond the bustling activity that surrounded me and saw someone standing at my bedside, not moving at all. It was a doctor. He stood looking at me, then looking away, then looking back at me.

"I am very sorry to have to tell you this, Mrs. Genzink. Your son Joshua has passed away."

In another room Ron was receiving the same news. "Your wife is badly hurt and your son has passed away."

"Oh, no, not Joshers," he moaned. "Oh no."

In my heart I knew it before the doctor said a word. After all, I was the one who'd told my son it was okay to go, to be with Jesus and Grandpa. Ironically, this is what Josh had wanted to do, had talked about, ever since my dad had died of a massive heart attack three years earlier. The passing of his grandfather had never been far from his mind. Only two weeks before the accident Joshua had asked Ron, "How does Jesus come down and get me, Dad? Does He have a ladder that comes down?"

Ron spent an hour talking to him at bedtime that night about how Jesus would bring us home. At the time we didn't think the conversation unusual, Joshua being such a deep thinker. He loved Jesus and talked about Him daily. His favorite song was "Jesus Loves Me."

I learned later that Joshua's head and chest had hit the dashboard during the accident. Though he was stable on the way to the hospital in the ambulance, he died soon after he arrived.

The news of our accident spread fast. Family friends came to the hospital, while others alerted our stunned babysitter. Still other friends came and got Misty and Deedee, and some of Ron's relatives took in baby Jordan.

Much of this I did not know at the time, though I remember our minister coming to the hospital and my
uncle Gerald putting a pillow behind one of my legs to
relieve the pain. I was not processing my surroundings
well. I lay alone in a dark room, waiting for my heart to
calm enough for them to take me into surgery on my hip
and femur.

Although my mother told me that nurses tried to put
my hip back in place and I screamed, I have no memory
of that. Apparently in the accident I hit the dash of our
station wagon with my face and knee. Besides my broken right hip and shattered left femur, I had a severely
damaged nose. Inside me more danger lurked. Silently,
two blot clots traveled from my heart to my lungs. It is
a miracle that I survived the accident and its aftermath.
Ron's injuries were serious, too, because of the way he
had ended up under the steering wheel. He had a broken
right tibia and one broken rib.

Details began to emerge about the cause of the accident. We were told that the man whose car had swerved
in front of us as he came home from a bar in nearby Saugatuck. It isn't clear whether he suffered a heart attack,
whether the road conditions caused him to lose control,
or whether the accident happened because his blood alcohol content was too high—someone told me his con-
centration was over 0.30. He was the first one to leave
the scene with emergency crew, and he died either on the
way to the hospital or at the hospital.

From the beginning, despite the pain, I was glad I
had been hurt in the accident. Somehow it made Josh's
death easier knowing that I had been hurt too. If I had to
suffer and experience pain, I could not think all the time.

The subsequent hours and days are blurred in my
mind because I was so heavily medicated. I underwent
multiple surgeries followed by intensive therapy. After
the surgeries, in which the doctors put a screw in my

right hip and a plate with fifteen screws in my shattered left femur, I had to lie in traction on my hip with weights pulling my leg down at the foot end of the bed. On the other leg, a machine constantly kept my knee and femur in motion. Any thought of being able to walk soon disappeared.

Incredible to say, when I had surgery on my nose and they packed it after it was set, it felt worse than my leg or hip surgery. I could not breathe. Food was tasteless to me, and the combination of pain and other medications took away my appetite. I lost about twenty pounds over the course of my recovery, coming close to the ninety pounds I'd weighed during high school.

I was given large doses of morphine, and when the doctors began to wean me off it I experienced hallucinations. The nurses telephoned my mom one time in the middle of the night because I was so frantic, and she tried over the line to calm me down. I told her that people were after me. I was running up a hill and they were chasing me. I was hiding everywhere and was scared they were going to find me. I kept telling her to be quiet so they would not hear us.

Mom just listened and talked softly to me to calm me, and my heart finally slowed down. After a few hours the nurse came back in and told my mom, who was still on the line, that I had fallen asleep.

We had another trial to undergo. The following Tuesday, November 21, was the visitation at the funeral home. Ron and I obviously were unable to attend, so my mom, our friend Ron, and my brother Dan and his wife Shelly represented us, along with my husband's family. What I know of that event came through those who attended it, as well as my precious copy of the program.

The visitation was only for one evening, and more than five hundred people attended, including family, friends, and most of the children from Josh's class and their parents. Because of the number of children who attended, the casket was kept closed, with a photograph of Joshua on top of the coffin.

That same day Josh's school had a memorial service for him during the school day. What do you tell children who just a week earlier were standing shoulder-to-shoulder with a child who is no longer there? The principal began by explaining to the students what a memorial service was—a way to remember someone and to ask God to help us through difficult times. Then all the children sang "Jesus Loves Me," Josh's favorite song, and Reverend Lont spoke to the children about how we can always get help from the Bible because it is God's Word.

God gave us life, he said, but that life does come to an end. At some time we will all die. He read Psalm 89:

Remember how fleeting is my life.
For what futility you have created all humanity!
Who can live and not see death,
or who can escape the power of the grave?

"We wanted Joshua to live longer," the minister said, "but God, who made Joshua, wanted him to be with him now. In Matthew 19:14, Jesus said, 'Let the little children come to me, and do not hinder them, for the kingdom of heaven belongs to such as these.'"

He turned to the children in attendance. "God loves children, he loved Joshua, and he loves you. It's a wonderful thing to sit on Mommy's and Daddy's laps. Joshua is no longer sitting on his mommy's lap but is sitting on Jesus' lap. It's okay to feel sad or cry that Joshua has died, but it is such a special thing that he is with Jesus. God is with you every day of your life. Every time you sing, remember Joshua and how happy he is that you are singing praises to God."

The program ended, I was told, with all the children singing "Heaven Is a Wonderful Place" and "God Is So Good."

The funeral was Wednesday, the next morning, and was held at the hospital so that Ron and I could attend. It was conducted in the hospital's dark, gloomy basement. Our minister, Reverend Dykstra of Graafschap Christian Reformed Church, urged us to attend because he felt we needed the closure of seeing the body of our precious Joshua, and our extended family accompanied us as with broken hearts all took one last look at his peaceful little body.

There wasn't much room, so for the most part only family attended. Our children Deedee and Jordan were too little so were kept at home. At the viewing at the hospital before the funeral, my mom held four-year-old Misty. She looked at her brother, and though she felt choked and couldn't talk much, she said she was not sad.

"But why are his lips so red?" she murmured.

Her absence of feelings mirrored mine, perhaps. To be honest, I do not remember crying or feeling anything. What I saw and experienced there seemed surreal. A nurse pushed me, still hooked up to all kinds of machines, down through the maze-like, echoing hallways in my hospital bed. I had no part in planning the funeral other than pointing out some clothes for Josh to wear. In our stead his family graciously selected the casket, the music and songs, the singer, the message and even the burial site.

Everyone attending sat waiting until someone pushed Ron in his wheelchair into the room. His leg was elevated, his head was down, and a white hospital blanket lay draped around his shoulders. He looked so solemn that I wanted to tell him, "Put your head up and greet these people who came to show love for our son and us."

For some reason it seemed to me as though I should act as a hostess to everyone who came, so I came in smiling and nodding to each person I passed, reaching out toward some of them. I can't imagine what they must have thought as they looked at me. I was pushed along in my bed with IVs and blood transfusion bags dangling around me, one leg in the motion machine and the other in traction. I was wearing a hospital gown, and my face and body were covered with black and blue bruises. My nose was smashed in. Everyone stared at me—out of concern and curiosity, I am sure—because Ron and I had been in the hospital for almost a week and a lot of those people had not yet seen us because we had been unable to attend the visitation.

We turned our attention to the ceremony. What does a minister say to such a group? Reverend Dykstra recited Psalm 23, which tells of the tender shepherding care of the Lord, and Psalm 100:

For the LORD is good, and His love endures forever,
His faithfulness continues through all generations.

He prayed for comfort for us, as well as for healing of the pain and sorrow we were going through, thanking God for sparing our lives and asking blessings on the doctors who would be taking care of us. Then he talked about Joshua: he had been praising the Lord the night he died, and now he was praising God in heaven.

Reverend Dykstra's sermon was on Isaiah 40, reminding us that Jesus is our shepherd and we are His sheep. Some of the phrases, even the familiar ones, took on a strange and terrible new meaning as I listened to them.

"The grass withers and the flowers fall off because of the breath of the Lord," he said. "We human beings are grass, and we will all wither; all our best-loved flowers will eventually fall. But there is a constant, the Word of our God that will never pass away."

Bill Rigg sang two songs, "He's Got the Whole World in His Hands" and "It Is Well With My Soul." When the last note sounded the cavernous basement was so quiet you could have heard a pin drop.

At that most inopportune moment, the alarm on my IV monitor sounded. I saw people startle. Some turned, but others did not dare.

"Hurry and fix that!" I directed my nurse, Jackie. "They're going to think I'm dying." It didn't seem strange to me to find humor at that moment. Humor and the grace of God kept me sane during that time.

Reverend Dykstra concluded with the reminder that we are God's sheep. "Not one hair falls from our head without Him knowing about it, because He watches over His sheep, cares for them, protects them," he said. "But He takes special care of the little lambs and holds them close to His heart. And we know without a doubt that Joshua is in heaven with Jesus."

He ended with a blessing over all of us, that we would find comfort in God's grace. And with the burial of our precious son, our firstborn child, a chapter in our lives came to an end.

Something came to an end inside me, too. I knew that I had to make some changes. I needed to surrender not to my circumstances but totally to God. The strong, controlling woman who could handle everything had to die, too. I had to let God come to be in charge of my life, to take over the devastation it had become.

And He did, and perfectly so. The coming days were rocky, but we were not alone. We had to live out the truth that we inscribed on Joshua's gravestone: Jesus Loves Me.

9

A Long Road Back

I have often wondered whether it was something I did that brought such a disaster onto our family. Not long before the accident I had prayed for patience, and the Lord answered my prayer perfectly. What He showed me I needed was time to be still, learning to trust Him. What a hateful place to have to learn this, in a hospital bed, unable to do almost anything for myself. I, who had effortlessly juggled so many tasks, now needed to rely on everyone else.

For the first time in my adult life I couldn't take care of my house or prepare food for those I loved. I couldn't sit with my children and give them baths and read them stories at bedtime, or any of the other tasks I loved so much. My conversations with my husband were all about medical issues and other looming problems.

Worst of all, I couldn't even take care of myself—I couldn't get up to go to the bathroom or walk anywhere at all. Confined to the small world of a hospital bed, I had to learn to trust others with all the important things in my life, including my own physical wellbeing.

My helplessness forced me to rely most especially on God. It drove me toward Him—and perhaps that is one of the most important roles of a shepherd when dealing with wandering sheep. I had to learn the truth of what is meant by "in His time and in His way." I struggled and fought against it, because His way was not the way I wanted. It was not the way I would have ever chosen. This was not the dream I had thought I saw in my future when I married Ron.

Slowly, painfully, I came to accept the reality that though I had not chosen the timing, the Lord had. The statistics on dying are one hundred percent: Everyone will die. It's not if, but when. And He alone decides that "when." In God's timing He was ready to take to Himself that precious boy, given to us as a delightful gift for five and a half years. And for all the joy Ron and I had experienced in renovating our dream house for our family, the refuge God provided for our son when He welcomed him home was beyond anything Ron and I could have given him.

I also came to see those brief years our son was alive as a kind of completeness, the finishing of a task, and the doing it well. I have found peace in knowing that according to God's estimation, Joshua had accomplished his purpose in this world, whatever it was, in just five short years.

Crises in my life don't come and go; they seem to linger and overlap. I think that is true for most people—we don't settle one situation and then go on to the next crisis. The loss of our son was still bittersweet in our hearts, but his funeral did not end our missing him. Meanwhile, medical issues came breaking into our lives like waves on the seashore.

Thanksgiving Day came, and I was still in the hospital, with threatening blood clots in my lungs from my heart. Because of all my broken bones that had caused the clots, I was administered blood thinner Heparin injections into my stomach. I also underwent a surgical procedure to insert an umbrella-like wire called a greenway filter near my jugular vein to prevent clots going through my heart, because my legs just kept producing them.

My mom expressed her anxiety when she learned that my doctors had never done this procedure before and were having to research how to do it during the insertion. I guess everyone fears taking a maiden voyage with a doctor trying a new procedure. For my part, I remember the fog of anesthesia and the anesthesiologist's urgent words, "You'd better stop! We're losing her!"

"One more time, I almost got it . . . *I got it!*" replied the surgeon.

Although my life was in danger and others, like my mother, were agonizing over the risks, I remember drifting off and thinking, "Everyone else is at home together celebrating the holiday, and I'm here . . ."

Ron and I began our stay at Holland Hospital in the sixth floor critical care unit, but as we improved we were moved to the fifth floor for the remainder of the time we were there. My favorite nurses were Jackie, a lady from our church, and Jean, an older lady who was much like a mom when my own couldn't be there. Her listening heart gave me great support and wisdom that was far beyond my twenty-nine years of life experience. I loved her for that.

As I improved I became more sensitive to my own vulnerabilities. I remember once when two or three nurses were in the hospital room giving me a bath and the door was left open. No curtain shielded me, and I lay there naked as they bathed me. Although I'd given birth to four children in a hospital with people watching, this felt different. I felt degraded and ashamed, and when a nurse asked what was the matter I could only shake my head as tears ran down my cheeks.

After a couple of weeks in the hospital, my boss from the beauty salon came and gave me a great service by shampooing my hair. This was a sober reminder of what had happened, and how part of it would continue to linger. As she tenderly washed my hair, blood and pieces of glass from our car windows came out of it. But what a difference it made in how I felt to have my hair clean of those things.

For the most part the hospital restricted visitors for Ron and me. I'm not sure why, but I think that my appearance and precarious health—and, of course, the immensity of our loss—might have been the reasons. Ron was released after three weeks, but he simply couldn't bear to go to our home without Joshua and me there, so he stayed with his brother Gary until I was released. One week later I returned to our home in an ambulance.

But it was hardly a return to our former lives. There I stayed in the living room, with my hospital bed in the middle where the table saw had once sat. My care required twenty-four-seven nursing because of the shots and other demands of my condition.

Friends and family supplied abundant amounts of food every day and came and cleaned our house and watched our children and helped with errands. They brought gifts and money and prayers and love. We could never have survived without such generous and selfless help.

Of course, there was a downside to having people in our home all the time. For me, the hardest part was not having any time alone. My servant-hearted friends all meant well, but I was embarrassed by some of my needs. For instance, I had to bathe and change clothes in front of everyone, take my shots and medications, and even use the bathroom in bed in sight of anyone who was there. I could hardly bear that.

At first I tried to participate with some instructions on housework, but it got to the point with so many people coming and going that after a while people were emptying the dishwasher while the dishes were still dirty. God gave me the wisdom to not say anything in such cases. I had to look at the hearts of the people who were serving us, not the details of what they were doing. I kept my sanity by accepting the help offered to me and not looking too closely.

I felt keenly the loss of time with my children. Other people were taking care of them. A friend kept DeeDee and Misty, and my sister-in-law watched Jordan. There I felt a particular pain—I'd breast fed my other children and was no longer able to do that with Jordan. But God gave us the gift of new friends, people who cared about us and wanted us to get better.

And I desperately wanted to get better—for my husband, for my children, for the people who had worked so hard to help us, and for myself. I clung to the truth of a Scripture from Psalm 91, doing as it says in the first verses: dwelling in a shelter God had formed around me in my hospital bed, resting in His comforting and healing shadow.

"Because he loves me," says the Lord, "I will rescue him; I will protect him, for he acknowledges my name. He will call on me, and I will answer him; I will be with him in trouble, I will deliver him and honor him."

The verses in Psalm 91 that follow these were hard to hold on to, given the fact that we had seen the face of death, but I kept believing, no matter how the circumstances appeared. I believed that if I was in His shadow, dwelling with Him, I could handle whatever came my way.

"With long life I will satisfy him and show him my salvation."

A great milestone came the day a therapist began to come to the house to help me begin to walk with a walker. He worked hard with me, and I loved him for it. But the impact of being vertical on a body that had not borne its own weight and had been mainly horizontal for weeks was overwhelming: The first time I stood up I passed out. To give my body the additional strength and support it needed, I was fitted with a brace from my hip to my ankle.

I traveled to all my doctor appointments by ambulance. One incident brought into focus how even such an innocuous thing affected our children. Seeing an ambulance in the driveway was not the symbol for them that it was for me. I saw it and thought of the upcoming improvements that would allow me to return to my productive life. But the sight of it made my children anxious and afraid. Once our sweet-natured Misty kicked the nurse because she believed she was taking me away from her, perhaps forever.

But week by week my body began to heal. If I had a photograph album of pictures of the progress, they would show me first in a hospital bed in the intensive care unit, and then in a regular room, and later in a hospital bed in our living room. Then a snapshot would show me struggling with a walker and finally with crutches that the doctor required I use for a year. I loved the mobility.

Perhaps there should have been a photo of my carrying Jordan in one arm while walking with the other on a crutch. I was stubborn and admit that I often did not follow the doctors' or therapist's instructions—but these challenges, and seeing my gradual improvement, gave me encouragement with God's help to keep on going.

The home therapy gave way to outpatient therapy at the hospital for both Ron and me. Ron regained skills fairly quickly, but it took about three years of therapy for me, two to three times a week. To everyone's surprise, and to God's credit, I now walk with no limp, and with my foot facing forward, not inward as it was at first. (If I had a nickel for every time I heard "Foot out!" during that time, I would be a rich woman.) I gained strength and began to get movement back in my legs.

At home I had to repeatedly bend my left knee to rip the scar tissue and increase mobility. This was excruciatingly painful. Once a therapist was coaching me in the movements and stopped. "You need to breathe!" she said.

I didn't know I'd stopped. With tears streaming down my face, each time I would give it one more try. But it didn't prove to be enough, and finally surgery was necessary to release the stubborn scar tissue. Perhaps this aspect of my injuries helps to remind me that in a catastrophic loss not everything can be "fixed" by our own personal efforts.

Although I'd been told I'd never be able to fully bend that knee, I can now not only bend it but even sit on it. I still keep the pins and screws extracted during the last surgery as souvenirs. They remind me of the cost of such a recovery.

Going to therapy made me feel as though I was working for something and seeing progress. It kept me busy, which helped me not to think so much. Some days I felt as though all I did was go to doctors' appointments and therapy sessions. But I was a fighter and wanted to get my body back as nearly as possible into the condition it had been in before the accident (though with enough extra bionic parts to set off airport alarms). And in the main I recovered my health and mobility.

One thing that didn't return to normal was my nose. The cartilage had been destroyed in the accident, and despite two surgeries this changed my appearance so much that I look like a different person. Except for losing my dear Joshers, this was the biggest loss I felt. I regret not taking the opportunity for a surgery that would have used a bone from my hip to reconstruct my nose, which to this day still causes sinus problems.

But of course during the course of trying to just become mobile and return to caring for my children and husband, such a surgery didn't seem essential at the time. I have learned that often all you can do, in an extended crisis, is to put out the biggest fires and hope that the others can be dealt with later.

Sometimes I look back at that terrible time in our lives while we tried to recover from the accident and the loss of our son, and I wonder why. Were these things necessary for us—to learn patience? I take inventory of what good was accomplished through that time. Through the worst of it I never felt closer to the Lord than when I knew He was holding me in the palm of His hand. He gave me the gift of His peace: I had no fear, no anger, no self-pity. I pushed myself to keep going and to get better every day and was very proud of the progress I made.

The children were a wonderful distraction; they were in school and involved in activities that, as our health improved, kept us busy. The Lord gave us everything we needed right at the time we needed it, whether it was strength for tomorrow or peace for that moment or grace to get through each day trying to achieve the healing to restore our health. Those things we were able to tackle. Many useful tasks became easier with the passage of time.

But there was still an empty chair at the table, and an empty little boy's bedroom. In fact, our house became emptier while Ron and I were in the hospital. Some of our well-meaning friends down took the pictures he'd drawn from the refrigerator door. They'd cleaned up his bedroom and put his special blanket away. I believe they wanted to spare us the emotional jolt of seeing those things. But just the opposite was the case because noticing the absence of such things only emphasized the absence of our precious little boy. Nothing was left the way *he* had left it.

I don't blame my friends for their loving actions. There are no magic formulas for what is right or wrong in such a situation. What is insulating or comforting to one family may be hurtful to another. And to be honest, it isn't easy to predict reactions.

No one can "get over" such a loss quickly. In fact, no one ever gets over the loss of a child. But gradually time begins to heal the wounds, and each new day brings recognition of blessings that begin to outweigh the pain.

I have learned what is important and what is not. I always used to have my house "just so," spic and span from top to bottom and everything in its place. Now I let all that go and spend more time with my children. I take time with them, listen to what they have to say, stop to observe them. I pick my priorities, let certain things go, take each day as it comes, and don't look to tomorrow. Sometimes this is hour by hour, and even minute by minute on some days.

Another thing the Lord gives us as we go through horrific circumstances is a growing ability to understand what someone else is going through, based on having been there our self. For example, we became friends with a couple, the Walcotts, whose two young children had been killed in a car accident. Of course there was a connection only soul-sufferers could feel; sharing that painful link entailed real healing for all four of us, both as couples and as parents dealing with the loss of a child. Our oldest daughter and their oldest spent a lot of time together and are still friends today.

For all the closeness we felt to some people, we experienced great distance from others. Some didn't know how to respond to us after our losing Joshua. I believe it was too painful for some who have stayed away even to this day. Others would choose another aisle in the grocery store because, I think, they didn't know what to say.

Church was difficult and awkward as I returned in a wheelchair. Everything had changed. Not having experienced such loss, other people had no idea how to respond, and I respected that. I believe I usually made them feel better because I could see in their faces their acknowledgement of how bad I felt for them. I always want to be a peacemaker, to have things go smoothly, and to look for the positive in situations. The hope and grace that the Lord gives me are the greatest gift I have ever received.

I know something that others may not yet have come to know. I see that God gave us Joshua as a gift to care for and that this gift was a great blessing to us. His timing in taking him to heaven, though painful to us, was perfect. The older I get, the more I think about James 1:12:

> Blessed is the man who perseveres under trial, because when he has stood the test, he will receive the crown of life that God has promised to those who love him.

My job is to continue on the path set out before me, to prepare myself and those I love for that crown of life. I am more and more ready each year to go to heaven and see Josh, along with my father and others who are already there. I know Joshua is with the Lord in heaven, wearing his crown of life. I can't wait to see him again.

Part Two

OUR PERFECT CHILD

10

SWEETNESS

You can ask any parent which is the "favorite" child in a family, and in almost every case the parent will reply that he or she loves every child equally. But favoritism comes out in many ways. It may be the best-behaved child who gets a "bye" when no one owns up to a broken dish. Or it may be the rebellious one who touches parents' hearts and causes them to yearn for soul-to-soul contact with the little renegade who, they find, is much like them. It might be the weakest or sickest child who tears at a parent's heartstrings.

You might even think that in our case, perhaps the child who is no longer there is the one the parent might love the most. When one cannot show love physically to a deceased child, it's normal to try to compensate by pushing out of memory any of that child's small shortcomings.

But in our case, if you asked any of our family members I am sure each would concur with a conclusion. We have one child who is perfect. Absolutely perfect.

The two years after the death of Joshua were consumed by recuperation. People don't realize that being disabled, even temporarily, is a full-time job. Ron's auto-mobile accident injuries were muddled together with his recovery from his cancers, and often it was hard to tell which we were dealing with.

For my part, I spent almost two years on crutches, but I took hope because I believed that our hardest times were in the rearview mirror. The promise of God that He intended good toward us was never in doubt in my mind or heart, and I looked forward to the hope and future that I read about in Jeremiah 29:11.

During those years the reality of the empty chair at the table, the empty little boy's bedroom, were con-stantly in our minds. We missed our little Joshers. We knew there would never be another young man like him. And while we knew that he could never be "replaced" in any sense, our whole family—Ron, I, and the children who could remember Josh—began to talk about having another child. I look back and recall the way we talked about it. We knew we could never replace Josh. But his passing left an emptiness, a void, we longed to fill.

At first the idea of another child seemed not only im-practical but perhaps even unwise, because of Ron's ten-uous health and my determined but still slow recovery. In many ways we were still dependent upon others for help with some aspects of daily life, though our indepen-dence seemed on the horizon.

It was a great day for Ron and me when, in the fall of 1991, we traveled with church friends and family in a mo-tor home to a Praise Gathering hosted by the recording artists the Gaithers in the Hoosier Dome in Indianapo-lis. Thousands of believers were there, praising God, and the experience was like cool water on our crisis-parched souls. We began to look to the future.

Ron and I spoke to each other about our desire to have another child. In many ways we were caught be-tween the biblical blessings of having many children and our own modern situation. Were those statements of blessing just for Old Testament times, we wondered? Would my childhood dreams of a large family—dreams I believed were within the will and promises of God—be put aside based on "practicality"?

One of the seminars offered at the Praise Gathering was by author Brennan Manning. He spoke about the transformation in the story of Don Quixote, a transformation brought about by the human touch of a person he calls Dulcinea. In his book *The Furious Longing of God*, Manning describes this:

> But then it is Dulcinea's turn to speak the words of *could-be*; words that dream against words like *unbeatable, unbearable, unrightable, unreachable, impossible* . . . He stumbles out of his bed reborn, recreated, renewed, healed. He is born again by the loving touch of Dulcinea's affirmation and to the end he will dream his impossible dream. The question is not can we heal? The question, the only question, is will we let the healing power of the risen Jesus flow through us to reach and touch others, so that they dream and fight and bear and run where the brave dare not go?

Ron and I turned and looked at each other. We knew we were embarking on a new phase of our lives, and that it would have great importance for us and for our family.

"If God gives us another child and it's a girl," Ron breathed in my ear, "her name will be Dulcinea." Dulcinea. *Sweetness.* The very name filled us with joy and hope. Within a month that sweetness began to take form, growing inside me. As with previous pregnancies, as it progressed I felt better and better. But I was also aware that this new child was developing inside a different body than had my other children, a body redefined by mending bones, repeated surgeries and therapies and illness. How would that body respond to the urgencies of labor and delivery? I wondered.

My fears were unfounded. After an hour and a half of labor, on September 5 (Labor Day weekend 1992), our Dulcinea charged into the world, almost eight pounds and twenty inches long. She was beautiful and alert, with dark, curly hair.

At her first check-up the doctor said, "I can't find a thing wrong with her."

His words disturbed me, but I replied, "Well, I hope not!"

From the beginning she represented family, and hope and new beginnings. It was as though she had been born knitted into a community, sharing the same birthday week with a cousin and three friends from church. The beginning of a new school year meant that Misty and Deedee got to have a star attraction at "show and tell." Little Jordan's excitement at having a new baby in the house was contagious.

In late October she was baptized. I remember the voices of the youth choir as they sang about all things working together for good for those who love God (Romans 8:28), and I remember this passage from James 5:7:

Be patient, then, brothers and sisters, until the Lord's coming. See how the farmer waits for the land to yield its valuable crop, patiently waiting for the autumn and spring rains.

We saw all the potential of such value in this child, who lifted herself up when lying on her stomach, who was just beginning to smile. Do all parents feel guilt when they look back at seemingly innocuous events and try to tie them to what came later?

Two events happened before Dulci Jean was two months old. First was the occasion of her DPT (diphtheria, pertussis, tetanus) inoculation. Previously an active, happy child with regular sleep patterns, Dulci seemed fussy and drowsy afterward. Also during her first few weeks of her life I allowed a local pest control company to spray our home, inside and out, for mice and spider control—something that seemed inconsequential at the time.

At about that time I was preparing items for sale for a local craft show and noticed that Dulci was much more fussy and agitated. I would hold her in my arms, and like other children who "startle" awake, she would jerk almost imperceptibly. "Just a little quirk of her personality," I thought at first, but as the jerking became more frequent I began to worry.

The events that soon followed took the form of a quest, as I look back. We had seen what God had done in healing Ron from two kinds of cancers. He had given us both strength to recuperate from a devastating car accident and the even more devastating loss of our beloved child. He had given us children and another child when no one said we could have them, and now we had this beautiful girl, sweetness itself. Surely He could heal her from whatever this was, and we could go on with our dream of a large, healthy family.

We took Dulci to a hospital where a CT scan showed normal brain activity. The EEG, however, told a different story.

"Those aren't startles," a doctor told us gravely. "Each of those is a little seizure."

We looked at each other.

"What is causing this? What can we do?" I asked.

"We don't know."

The doctors at our local hospital referred us to a specialist in Grand Rapids, and for the first time with all our experiences with doctors we found out what it was to deal with an unsympathetic medical person. The first thing we noticed was his brusqueness in dealing with his staff.

"I don't want to talk to that patient," we heard him say about someone who was calling him. "Just keep the riff raff away from me."

We swallowed hard and allowed him to run some tests, anxious to hear the results. After all, he was an expert. In his office we sat across from him at his desk. He told us offhandedly that he didn't know what was causing the seizures and did not know of a treatment.

"What can we do?" I was crying. "Is there someone else we can consult?"

The sound of his chair back hitting the wall reverberated as he rose and towered over us. "So you don't trust me? Don't trust my opinion?" he exploded. "Go ahead and try to find someone else, then."

We weren't going to be deterred by his volatile reaction. We made an appointment for Dulci at the Mayo Clinic in Rochester, Minnesota. By this time she was eight months old, with no relief of her symptoms.

She was our child, and we wanted her to be healthy and well and perfect like all our other children. We would go to the moon and back to help her and make her well, so a nine-hour road trip with two children under the age of three, and four or five days of testing, seemed a small price to pay.

The tests involved X-rays, more EEGs, CT scans, examinations by an eye specialist, and blood work. Through all of this testing Dulci was a little trooper. When all the tests were over we again sat in a doctor's office anxiously waiting for results, explanations, treatments. Jordan sat quietly, looking at a book. Dulci was in her stroller. Ron and I were expectant, leaning across another desk in another office for some hope. But once again medical science had no answers for us.

"Take her home and live with her this way," the doctor said. We walked out of that office, feeling numb, and returned to our hotel room to pack our belongings. On the way home we stopped at a park alongside the Mississippi River and stood at its shore, trying to sort out our feelings. Dulci looked, blinking, at the water, and Jordan fed the ducks.

Ron and I reached out into the water. There, river-smoothed rocks were just within our reach. But when we held them, glistening in our hands, they were as mute as God about what we were to do about our precious daughter.

We continued our quest to restore Dulci to health. At home, our pediatrician offered a new treatment for the only diagnosis we have ever received regarding Dulci—"infantile spasms."

"It's new—an injection called ACTH," the doctor explained. "I wish we'd known about it when she first started the seizures. Now that she has gone this many months, I don't know if they will work."

We were more than willing to try, and I began the painful and traumatic ritual of learning how to prevent air bubbles in injections and how to administer them daily. Dulci would cry, and I would too. In the end it seemed to have no effect; to the contrary, she became ill and had to be hospitalized for a week.

Perhaps less aggressive and more natural techniques might help, advised a kinesiologist. On his advice I began taking special vitamins that would pass through my breast milk, and allowed him to adjust my posture as she lay on my stomach.

We continued to work with the Detroit Children's Hospital. They, with us, continued to look for a cure.

"Let's try a stronger dose of the ACTH," advised a doctor one day.

"Let me think about that," I replied. I went home and talked it over with Ron. I couldn't escape the sense that I shouldn't give her this medication again. As it turned out, that was precisely right. Within a few days, on December 18—the day the shots were scheduled—Dulci's weakened immune system succumbed to chicken pox, which in her fragile condition lasted over a month. Had she been undergoing those rigorous shots, the doctor told me, she should not have survived.

But she was destined by God to survive, and not just to continue going from one illness to the next. He was causing all things to work together for her good, as her baptismal Scriptures had promised. He was giving her, too, a future and a hope. And she, who could not move, was "stepping" into a role in our family that none of us could have imagined.

11

THE CLOSING OF A GREAT DOOR

We continued our quest for a way to restore our daughter to what we believed to be her intended health and potential. But no one in the medical community gave us hope. "Enjoy her," one doctor said gently. "She won't live to be ten years old, so enjoy her time now."

One day our church, the Graafschap Christian Reformed Church, decided to host an event to celebrate the lives of our congregation's children. One child per birth year was chosen, and we were thrilled that the year 1992 was to be represented by our Dulcinea Jean. With my help, Dulci "carried" a red rose signifying her year to the front of the church.

With my voice full of emotion, I read the poem that Ron had written for his daughter. Perhaps because of that event and its significance, I began to see Dulci in a different way. We had no intention of giving up our pursuit of answers and treatments for her, though.

"Perhaps the secret might lie in physical and occupational therapy," one medical professional suggested, but continued seizures kept her from making progress. So for weeks we took her to people who would stretch and coax her little muscles and limbs. For a while the seizures would stop, and we would think things were moving in a positive direction; but then they would come back, seemingly more ferocious than before.

"We're so sorry. We need to stop this therapy because we're not making any progress," we would hear. For six months this pattern continued: no answers, more seizing, more doctors, more medication, more praying.

In May of 1994 Dulci was nearly two. She began suffering from a cough and a fever, and as with any illness she had contracted, the seizures increased in number and intensity. Once in the hospital, she had another close call. An inattentive nurse in the emergency room, in a hurry perhaps, rushed an injection of phenobarbital. My mother was holding Dulci, and she went limp and passed out.

"You could have killed this child!" a doctor admonished the nurse. Although we knew that Dulci was under God's protection, such incidents highlighted in our minds just how fragile she was. But He brought another blessing to light when the blood tests revealed that Dulci had a type of pneumonia, perhaps brought on by aspirating food or her own fluids during the intensity of the seizures.

"Her white blood counts are so low we're testing her for leukemia," the doctor said, after examining her. "I think she should be transferred to another hospital where they can better address this."

As I rode in the ambulance with Dulci, so many memories flooded back. The last time I'd taken a ride in such a vehicle I was seriously injured and in horrible pain, and the fates of my husband and son was unknown to me. As

I looked at Dulci, pale and vulnerable, I wondered what lay ahead of us.

We spent a month in that Grand Rapids hospital. I sat in the chair next to her bed, her room a whirl of activity the whole time. First they performed a swallow test with a dye to determine how she was aspirating, and finally inserted a feeding tube into her nose. This was followed by countless needle sticks and IV insertions, chest X-rays and EEGs and oxygen therapy, a nebulizer and respiratory therapists who pounded on her back to make her cough, the dreaded suction machines and even a vibrating vest.

All of this was necessary, they explained, to help her recover from the pneumonia so that they could perform a surgery they believed would help with the aspiration. In a three-hour procedure called a Nissen Fundoplication surgery they wrapped the top of her stomach around her esophagus. As I sat anxiously in the waiting room, I comforted myself with the thought that perhaps she would be able to eat normally now.

"We're done with the surgery," the doctor said, pulling his mask down to his chest. "Everything went well. And of course the feeding tube is inserted, too, so perhaps this will help her get the nutrition she needs."

I was stunned. Feeding tube? I hadn't heard this part discussed before. Now Dulci would not eat any more at all—her food would go directly into her stomach via an implanted gastric tube. Next to me Ron nodded off to sleep, and my mother and I chatted with some of the others in the waiting room.

I was trying to deal with the profound disappointment I felt. Our sweet and innocent child had experienced yet another setback. I was simmering in my frustration when my mother's conversation with another woman finally hit me with nearly the physical impact of being struck with a baseball bat. This woman's son was also in surgery, and it would last nine hours. Whereas we faced upcoming challenges, we were assured the procedure would make things better for Dulci. This woman had no such hopeful prognosis.

This put our situation into a startling perspective. There was always someone else whose sorrow is more acute than mine. There was always a situation where there was less hope than my own. I needed that understanding to face the coming hours.

"She's just beautiful," a nurse assured me as Ron and my mom and I entered the room where Dulci was to stay after her surgery. And it was true—her color was rosy, and she began to be more alert. But soon the anesthesia began to wear off, and she was in terrible pain. I could hardly bear to see her that way. I felt so helpless.

Finally she began to respond to the pain medications and to her healing body. A new seizure medication helped to keep her calm, and technicians trained me in the particulars of how to administer her food with a bolus apparatus that used gravity to propel the food through the tube, or with a mechanical pump.

In a way this new phase for us was like the closing of a great door. For the first time we understood that this would be how Dulci would receive her nutrition for the rest of her life. This sobered us. Although the formulation of the liquids has changed as she has aged, the method has not.

But as she was getting better, I was noticing that I wasn't feeling well. Food didn't appeal to me. At first I wondered whether this had to do with handling the feeding tube and its products. Surely they are not designed to be visually appealing in any sense.

It wasn't long after that when I ordered a pizza and sat alone in the room with Ron. "I have some good news," I said brightly. His mouth was full. He looked at me suspiciously.

"We're going to have another baby." I began to smile, thinking of my dream of a dozen children. Although there were many challenges in taking care of Dulci, I was thrilled when I learned that another child was on the way.

He looked around the room in frustration. "With Dulci Jean in this condition, how could that be good news?" We both became accustomed to the idea, however, and it seemed more manageable as we transitioned into the summer months. We spent six weeks camping at Triponds Family Camp Resort in Allegan. Spring-fed lakes washed peace and comfort into our souls. The sunshine and trees reminded us of a God who provides for us even when we aren't aware of when or how He is doing so.

Best of all was seeing how this affected Dulci. True, she still functioned as a two or three month-old child. She still couldn't walk or talk or even sit alone or hold her head up. But with gentle, lake-born breezes caressing her cheeks, amidst the laughter of other children, she surrendered herself to everything that was around her, and her peaceful expression told us that she had not a care in the world that was created by such a God.

Our Angel
by Ron Genzink

An Angel came one September day
thank you Lord for this precious girl we prayed
with your beautiful eyes of blue
but you can't see like others do
with your cute little brown curls
you are the third of three pretty girls
but at such an innocent age
there came a drastic change
for years you made little progress
even days you laid motionless
as you seem to go downhill

it was hard to think it was God's will
they say you will never sing or dance
and if so just by chance
on earth maybe you can't run or play
but we know you will someday,
it hurts to hear your painful cry,
but what a joy your gentle sigh,
we may never know why,
you can't see the gentle butterfly,
or why you can't walk,
or why you can't talk,
no one will ever understand,
the feelings when you hold our hand,
some people stop and stare,
but as for us, we don't really care,
with all the things you can or cannot do,
you make us so very proud of you,
with little progress you make,
we know you're not a mistake,
we were once told, that you would never grow old,
but little the doctors knew,
what our awesome God can do,
we prayed for miracles that would never come,
but we know you yourself are one,
you will probably never win a race,
until you see Jesus face to face,
now we put our faith and trust,
into the One who gave you to us,
you may never know how much to us you mean,
our precious, precious, daughter, Dulci Jean.

My mother, Audrey Allen, and me. Summer of 1961. I was born August 19, 1960.

My brother and me at the lake lot,
on the go-cart my dad made, in August 1972.
I am twelve and my brother is nine.

Proud first-time home owners, May 1981.
I am sweeping our front porch.

Ron and me.
Our engagement photo.
July 1981.

My father, Dee Dexter Allen,
on his horse, Blue.
Summer 1981.

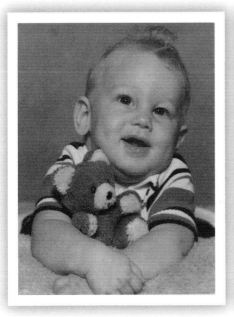

Joshua Jay—Joshers—at six months old, 1984. Born February 28, 1984.

Joshua, May 1985, during Holland, Michigan's Tulip Time festival in his Dutch costume in Grandma Allen's backyard.

Joshua, Ron, and me, summer 1984. Ron's hair is growing back after his radiation. Treatment was complete, and there had been a dramatic improvement. No more tumor!

Ron with Joshua, six months old, at Ludington State Park, August 1984.

Melista Dee (Misty) at seven months,
February 1986. Born July 6, 1985.

Joshua and me after my dad's death on
October 15, 1986. Joshua is looking up
toward heaven.

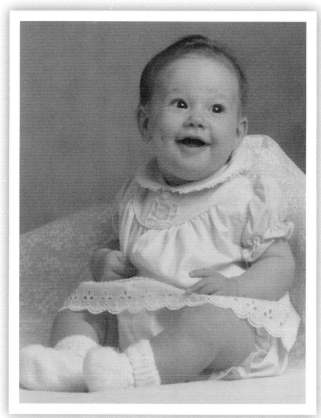

Deidre Nicole (DeeDee),
three months old,
June 1987.
Born March 23, 1987.

Myself, Josh, and Misty on a hot summer day in our home in 1988.

Josh and Misty making popcorn in our home—never one without the other. February 1989.

Josh, Misty, and DeeDee
in the spring of 1989.
Ages four, three,
and two.

Jordan at 12 months,
summer 1990.
Born August 2, 1989.

Joshua's school picture,
taken October 1989.
He was five-and-a-half
years old.

Icy road blamed for collision that killed driver, kid

HOLLAND

By Jon Brandt
The Grand Rapids Press

Five-year-old Joshua Genzink was returning home with his parents from a school program late Friday when another car slid into their lane on an icy road, according to Allegan County sheriff's deputies.

Joshua and the driver of the other vehicle, Harvey J. Wolters, 59, of Holland, were killed in the accident on Blue Star Highway in Fillmore Township.

Joshua's parents, Ronald and Lavonne Genzink, of A3768 58th Ave., Holland, were listed in good and fair condition, respectively, Saturday at Holland Community Hospital.

"He was a real loving, loving child," said Heamina Genzink, Joshua's grandmother.

Joshua's grandfather, Arnold Genzink, said his son's family was returning from Central Wesleyan Church where Southside Christian School, including Joshua's kindergarten class, put on a school program.

"He just stood up there singing his praises to the Lord," Arnold Genzink said.

Joshua was the oldest of Genzinks' four children. None of the other children — Melista, 4, Diedre, 2, and Jordan, four months — was in the car.

The accident occurred at 10:50 p.m. Friday under snowy and icy conditions.

Allegan County Sheriff's Department officials said Wolters, of 52 Old Mill Drive in Holland, was traveling northbound on Blue Star Highway when his vehicle apparently slid sideways into the southbound lane.

The Genzink vehicle, driven by Ronald, was traveling southbound on Blue Star and hit Wolters' vehicle in the passenger side.

Ronald Genzink was pinned in his automobile until Graafschap Rescue personnel could free him, according to police reports. Nobody in either vehicle was wearing seatbelts, police said.

Although the accident remains under investigation, officials said an icy roadway was a "major contributing factor."

Wolters was declared dead on arrival at Holland Community Hospital.

He is survived by his wife, Norma; four children, Ronald and Susan Wolters, Michael and Judith Wolters, Douglas and Beth Kooiker, all of Holland, and Elaine Wolters of Zeeland; six grandchildren; one stepson, Michael Cotts of Holland; one stepdaughter, Karen Lindeman of Orlando, Fla.; five brothers and one sister.

Wolters owned and operated HiLo Auto Sales in Holland for 30 years.

Services for Wolters will be held 1 p.m. Tuesday at Notier-Ver Lee-Langeland Chapel, with burial at Graafschap Cemetery.

Visitations will be held 7-9 p.m. Monday at the chapel.

Funeral arrangements for Joshua Genzink were incomplete.

Newspaper article posted
day after accident on
November 18, 1989.

Our red station wagon after the accident.

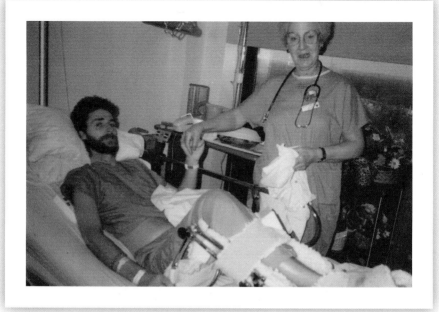

Ron in the hospital after the accident with a broken tibia and ribs.
He is being cared for by our favorite nurse, Jean.

Misty, and DeeDee
visiting me in the hospital
after the accident.
December 1989.

First family picture
after Josh's death,
summer 1991.

Dulcinea Jean (Dulci),
born September 5, 1992.
Here she is in the hospital
in May of 1994 with
Jordan, DeeDee,
and Misty.

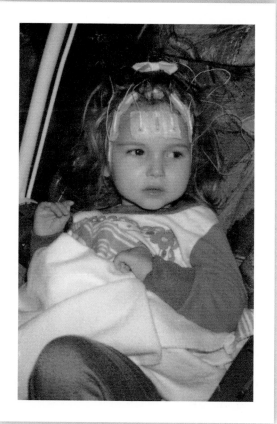

Dulci in stroller at the hospital
getting an EEG in summer
of 1994—trying to figure out
why she has seizures.

Ron's father and mother, Arnie and Hermina Genzink, October 1994.

My mom, Audrey Allen, Summer, 1995

Isabella Rose (Belle)
at 20 months old
in October 1996.
Born February 2, 1995.

Mercedes Grace (Sadie)
at 18 months old
in December 1999.
Born May 21, 1998.

'He still gets to be a kid'

◻ Teen struggles to lead normal life as he battles disease, awaits transplant

By LESA INGRAHAM
Staff writer

Jordan Genzink just wanted to play basketball with his fellow eighth-graders.

But, a rare illness is keeping him off the court.

In January, when Genzink was playing on a Holland Christian basketball clinic, he didn't feel well.

After a few trips to the doctor, the 14-year-old's swollen ankles led doctors to a diagnosis of potentially fatal kidney failure.

The diagnosis couldn't have come at a worse time, with Jordan's father Ron losing his job days before and his grandfather dying soon after.

Jordan's mother Vonnie said if it wasn't for her faith, she doesn't know how she would cope with everything that has happened.

"You have to look at the good things in life. When Ron's father died the whole family came and it was nice, because the whole family is never together," she said.

Learning how to cope isn't new to the Genzink family, with Ron having battled cancer twice and the couple losing their oldest son, Joshua, when he was 5 because of a drunken driver.

Things aren't going as planned for Jordan this summer, spending 12 hours a day on a dialysis machine. But, he said he still gets to be a kid.

"Even though I'm doing all this, I still get to have some fun," Jordan said while camping with his family in Allegan.

He said he is feeling better, now that he is being treated.

"At first, I just didn't feel good, but I'm feeling much better. I think the dialysis a wig," Jordan said.

With Jordan spending a month in the hospital in Ann Arbor because there aren't facilities in West Michigan to treat him and monthly trips to the doctor, the medical bills are piling up.

"This weekend and for a reason, when I needed Ron to be home, he was home because he lost his job late in May. Jordan got out of the

HOLLAND

hospital, Ron got his job back. This worked out well, because he was home when I needed him to be and then back to work when he really needed the money," Vonnie said.

To help combat some of the costs, Mike Lamence, who goes to church with the Genzinks, is hosting a fund-raiser. On Aug. 12, Holland businesses, Quality Oil Change, 1200 James St., Quality Car Wash, 809 S. Washington, 499 E. 8th St. and 345 S. River are teaming up to raise funds, according to Lamence.

For the entire day, $10 from each oil change completed and $1 for each car wash will go toward medical-related expenses for the family.

Right now, Vonnie isn't sure of or when Jordan will be able to receive a transplant.

"I am going to be tested, to see if I'm a match, but my husband can't do it because he's had cancer and our five younger children — he has five younger sisters and they are too young. If I'm not a match, then he'll be put on a waiting list and it could be six months to a year," Vonnie said.

Jordan's sisters, Misty, DeeDee, Dalel, Belle and Sadie, range in age from 5 to 18.

But, regardless of the wait, Vonnie remains optimistic that things will work out.

"I'm so happy for our church and our family and friends. They've really been there for us," Vonnie said.

Even with the transplant, Jordan won't be able to return to the football field or basketball court, but at least he'll be alive and healthy, Vonnie said.

PORTABLE: *Jordan Genzink, 14, poses with his portable kidney dialysis machine. When his family goes camping, Jordan takes the machine right along with them.*

Jordan was interviewed by our local news station, WoodTV 8, while we were camping at Tri-Ponds, and an article was placed in our local newspaper, *The Holland Sentinel*, in the summer of 2004 after he was diagnosed with kidney failure. Jordan is photographed with the dialysis machine we took along with us camping.

Jordan playing rocket football in 2000. He was coached by Walter Lamb, who became a great mentor to him. He is 11 years old here.

Jordan Lee getting wheeled into the operating room to get his new kidney! January 1, 2007. The grin on his face was priceless.

Family picture for our church directory, summer 2007.

Dulci at age 15 in December 2007.
Isn't she beautiful?

Dulci swimming with her caregiver, Rachel,
summer 2010.

DeeDee and Derek DeFrell,
married June 4, 2011.

Misty and Jordan Sligh,
married September 28, 2012.

Christmas, 2012.
Dulci's caregiver surprised us
with pictures of Dulci.

Dulci at Mary Free Bed Hospital trying out her new bike,
March 2013.

Belle playing softball
spring 2013.
She played third base.

Sadie playing tennis,
spring 2013.

Ron and me at a friend's wedding,
October 2013.

Jordan and Erin Genzink,
married May 10, 2013.

Our whole family at Erin and Jordan's wedding. Front row: Dulci, Maxwell.
Back row: Jordan Sligh; Misty; me, Ron; my mother, Audrey Allen; Jordan; Erin; Belle;
Sadie; DeeDee; Derek DeFrell.

Our greatest blessings! Misty, Sadie, Jordan, DeeDee, Belle, and Dulci.

12

TEACHING WITHOUT WORDS

We were parents. We loved our Dulci. And so we kept trying to find ways to help her improve. In December we took her to the Cleveland Clinic. She spent a week with monitoring video EEGs and more tests. One involved numbing the skin of the arm, removing part of the skin as a biopsy, and sewing it back up. Other tests depended on blood samples, and this was painful and frustrating because it is so difficult to get blood from Dulci on the first, . . . or tenth, or even twentieth "stick."

We got good news from the spinal puncture—the fluid was clear, which precluded a great many conditions. But most trying of all were the tests on her eyes. Understandably, Dulci hates having anyone try to examine any part of her face. But they were able to numb and dilate her eyes and perform an ERG that would depict what the cornea could see. We were disappointed to learn that Dulci cannot see as other people do. It's as though she is looking from the end of a long tunnel, and she has no peripheral vision. Some of the other tests I was not able to attend because of the potential danger to the baby I was carrying inside me.

We went home after all those tests with no more treatment options that we'd had before. Again, the only advice was to take her home and love her, because we had only a few more years to spend with her. And so we loved her, all the while preparing for our newest family member.

Our daughter Isabella, or Belle, as we call her, came into the world on February 2, 1995, born on Jordan's half birthday. She was beautiful, the happiest and most contented baby, always smiling. She brought us peace after so much sickness with Dulci. Belle was, and still is, our "joy" everyday.

By September our three-year-old Dulci passed a major milestone. She was enrolled in school. A bus came to pick her up every day, and she loved the bouncing motion of the bus itself. She spent all day Tuesdays and Thursdays with a special teacher and two paraprofessionals. From her contented expressions each day when she returned, we could see that this was an enjoyable experience for Dulci.

Another doctor suggested a ketogenic diet for Dulci. We traveled again to Detroit, where Ron checked into a Ronald McDonald House, while I stayed in the hospital with Dulci. The idea was to change her tube feeding to a substance that was very high in fat. This would deplete Dulci's body of all glucose and force it to exist on fat alone, which could greatly reduce the number of her seizures. Unfortunately, this strategy met with no success.

Once again I was feeling sorry for ourselves and for Dulci. And then the baseball bat of comparison hit me again. To gain perspective, all I had to do was look around: next to us was a tiny patient named Aubrey. She had an undersized brain and was blind, mentally disabled, and constantly choked, having to be suctioned.

There is always someone whose situation is worse than ours, I remembered.

Our final attempt in the quest for answers came when we shuttled through a string of pediatric neurologists. One, Dr. Liza Squires, patiently worked through every available seizure medicine to try to find a combination that would help Dulci. Finally we found a mixture that seemed to work better than any other.

Dulci, within the parameters of who she is and what she could do, passed several important milestones as she grew. In December of 1995 she was fitted for her first wheelchair. The next year she took her first ride on a horse. Later she would have her first dentist appointment and, like all children, lose her first tooth.

But while she was moving past the milestones of babyhood, I still yearned for another child. On my birthday in August of 1997 I asked Ron for one more child. He used to joke that when he would lay his trousers across the bed I would become pregnant; that very night Mercedes Grace was conceived.

Dark complexioned and with black hair, our newest girl was born on May 21, 1998. Naming her Mercedes was our private joke: We knew we'd never be able to afford the luxury car by that name, so we "made" one instead.

As she grew, the other children took to calling her "the little orphan" because she dressed with mismatched abandon and never cared whether her clothes were dirty or clean. Ron and I called her Sadie, and DeeDee mothered her as much as I did. When this talkative toddler—who used words like "actually" when she was three years old—would tire, I would find Sadie and DeeDee in each other's arms, asleep on the couch or wherever they dropped off in slumber.

Meanwhile, Dulci continued to achieve things no one had ever dreamed she could. She was an "ice skater" in a school Christmas program and took part in a Tulip Time parade, part of an annual festival in Holland, Michigan. She's been a flower girl and a bridesmaid in her sisters', brother's, cousins', friends' and caregivers' weddings. She went to summer camp and was able even to stay overnight with a respite caregiver. She was included in a night of square dancing and wagon rides, a day in the pool, games, a talent show, Special Olympics activities, and camping out under the stars.

And she loved every single moment of it. She even went to her first school prom.

At the age of eighteen she stopped going to school not because she didn't love it but because she would contract every virus and flu that went through it. The time had come for her to stay home to protect her health. So in-home caregivers came and helped with Dulci—bathing her, taking her to doctors' appointments and out into the community. They did exercises; helped her with her vibrating vest; fed her; and, as we did, loved her. The predictions of her dying before she was ten certainly haven't come true—she will be twenty-two in 2014.

There have been ups and downs. More discoveries and more disappointments. More hospitalizations and more tiny triumphs. But perhaps the most important landmark of her life occurred when she turned five years old. This wasn't a transition for her but for all the rest of us.

Ron and I finally realized something: for five years we'd been trying to "fix" our daughter. We, on our Don Quixote quest for our Dulcinea, had tried everything we could do to make her well, to stop her seizures, to make her like our other children. We jumped at every option put before us, tried every doctor and hospital and treatment and drug and diet that was proposed, to find out what was causing her constant seizures. We jousted at the windmills. And they were full of wind and vanity.

In the final analysis, there simply were no answers. She ages with us, accumulating now over twenty years of experience in life, but processing it now and always as an infant in an adult's body.

"She is perfect, just the way she is," God told us. Of course we still take her to doctors for her checkups and follow their advice to control the seizures—but with the certain knowledge that our daughter is, and always has been, a perfect gift from God. She is His child. We are content with her and have finally accepted that she is perfect. He doesn't make any mistakes.

We never did anything to try to change her after that. In fact, she has changed us. Our love for her, if it has done anything, has kept her alive, because we as a family love her more than life itself. She has taught our family so much. We understand people with disabilities, and not just how to observe and relate to them.

Every one of my other children has been involved in camps and school and youth and adult homes to take care of other Dulcis, young and old, with their special needs. Even though Sadie, still in high school, is involved in cheerleading and tennis and other activities, she has a heart for service.

Misty is a social worker, an amazing one. Deedee chose as her life profession to be a special education teacher—one who understands things a school alone could never teach. Jordan became involved with Youth With a Mission (YWAM), and Belle is transitioning to a pre-seminary program. Each one of our other children has chosen a career and activities that are other-centered and service-rich. Dulci, who has never spoken a single word, is our teacher. We thank the Lord every day for her and the love and blessing we have received because God gave her to us.

I remember one time when Dulci was undergoing the tests at the Cleveland Clinic. Ron and I were walking through the cafeteria, pushing Dulci in her stroller, killing some time between procedures. A man walked up to us, bent over, and looked into the stroller. "Where are her wings?" he asked.

"Her wings?" I asked. Ron and I looked at each other for a moment. Our angel.

We smiled broadly at the man, who nodded with satisfaction at our answer: "They are tucked underneath her right now."

13

A Grand Collaboration

I am a joyful person. My life is filled with happiness, satisfaction and fulfillment. Our home has had tragedy and challenges enter into it, but it is still a structure of joy. Other people see it and comment on it. There are reasons why our lives and our home are joyous.

One factor is something for which I can take no personal credit. I think that in childhood God gave me a sunny disposition because He knew I would need it in adulthood. But when I was a little girl I wanted to please everyone. I was quiet and shy and shrank from any kind of confrontation. I was serious-minded and never wanted to cause my parents worry or trouble.

I think something changed about me and the way my parents saw me the day I got lost trying to walk home from my friend's house and ended up across town near my dad's work. Dad's words to me—that if I could handle a situation like that without being scared I could handle anything—made me think of myself differently.

I can still remember my mother's frightened, angry face that day (as a mother myself, I certainly understand now!). And some of her worries came true—from that point on I became fearless, and that isn't always a good thing for a young girl. I was always respectful of my parents, but I gained a stubbornness that complemented that fearlessness.

But I also remember Dad's big smile and his ringing laugh of approval, both of which have stayed with me my whole life. He had faith in me. He trusted me. He was proud of me. I never wanted to lose that. With each new challenge in my life, I still hear my father's voice in my ear, cheering me on, even though he is no longer alive. He told me that with God's help I could face anything.

I see that mirrored in my faith in God. With Him I know I can't go wrong. With Him I will always be taken care of. I have the "peace that passes understanding" of which Scripture speaks; I can do "all things through Christ who strengthens me." What builds my faith is my father—and my heavenly Father, who loves me, believes in me and tells me even now that I can do anything.

I have no doubt that my children see that faith, a gift from both fathers, and I want to pass it along to them. I think I do that best when they see me confident and trusting in God. That is the single best legacy I can offer them.

My mom and dad gave me a gift of which I often speak with my children. "My parents put a little voice in my head that tells me to do a right, good thing or to turn away from a wrong course of action," I tell my children. "I can hear that voice from them ringing in my ears and in my head, and it has become a part of my conscience."

Apparently this is an inherited trait, because my children—especially Jordan—often say that they can hear my voice, or my mother's, ringing in their heads during times of decision.

My mother is still my protector and my rock. She reminds me all the time that I should take care of myself, that if I don't do that I can't take care of others—but her extravagant love and faith have been my example. She was the youngest of seven children and saw her oldest sibling, her own father, and her husband precede her in death. But she wanted to serve and help, and she took care of all of her brothers and sisters as they aged (or died violently, as in the case of one sister and a sister-in-law who passed away in a horrific car accident).

She knows pain. She knows how to survive and rise above circumstances. She is a role model and a sounding board not just for me but for our children as well. I know that I have suffered the loss of my son and my father, along with cherished childhood dreams. But honestly, the one thing I don't know how I could bear would be the loss of my mother.

I wonder sometimes when I hear others say that they couldn't bear what I have undergone. But I cling to the fact that God assures us that with Him anything is possible. Any loss of a loved one is bearable (even that of my mother, I know). Any financial struggles are bearable. Any dashed dream can be surmounted. I know we want to believe that, but the reality for most of us is that it is very hard to make those promises of God a reality in the face of the empty chair, the empty bank account, the empty future.

In such situations we tend to think about what we have lost instead of about what we still have, which is hope—without God, a treasure that would be utterly inconceivable in a devastating situation. If I can't see what that hope is going to produce in the future, I search for and gaze upon what it is producing right now.

Silently and sometimes without our even knowing it, suffering produces perseverance. We learn how to put one foot in front of the other and to lift up our faces to the sun. Only faith in God and in his changeless character can help us do that. If we don't trust Him, if we suspect His motives or the extent of His power, we can't look up. That perseverance does indeed build character, as Romans 5 reminds us.

I don't want to be prideful when I speak of our children. But anyone who knows them sees their character. These children have grown up in the oddest, most challenging set of circumstances, and yet they have learned the inestimable value of a great character trait: the desire to protect.

The best example is the way they have always related to little Dulci. When she first started having seizures she did not like to be touched. One doctor told me that this must have felt to her like needle pricks all over her body. The only solution was to soothe her and get her used to being touched. We would take turns gently rubbing her down, all over her tender little shoulders and chest and back and head and limbs, to get her used to being held and to acclimate her skin to contact. (Does she love it? Today, if you pick her up and hold her close to you, your legs will lose circulation long before she's ready to be put down!)

I had two other children after Dulci. She would lie on the floor while the babies crawled all over her—and she loved it. Of course she would get hit or kicked accidentally, but those were moments when we could teach the little ones about how to be gentle. My children, even as young as two years old themselves, would wipe her drool as though this were nothing and would learn to feed her through a tube.

All of the children participated in changing her diapers and, as I've indicated, even learned how to help with her tube feeding. They learned to be aware of the condition of someone else, to recognize the signs of a seizure, and to know what they could do to limit its severity.

One of our favorite stories involved our all-boy Jordan, whom we once sent in to check on Dulci as she slept.

He came out yelling at the top of his lungs that she had somehow managed to fall off the bed. He knew something was wrong and took his job as monitor very seriously. He was going to get someone's attention no matter what it took!

All of the children were and are proud of what they've learned. They all tenderly loved Dulci. When we would go out in public, I observed with fierce pride their care over her. Even the littlest ones without another thought would move to cover Dulci to conceal her from people who might stare or make insensitive remarks.

I think that's because we all recognize the truth of what Jesus said when He told us that when we care for "the least" among us we are taking care of Him. And the love and joy we've learned from Dulci we surely could never have learned from anyone else. She shows us the love of Jesus and His work without saying a single word. She can't talk, walk, eat, or even sit by herself. And yet she witnesses to us what it is like to be silent and accept whatever someone does to you. She never complains. Imagine having in your midst someone who never does anything wrong—in mind or in action. Imagine having the example of sinlessness always with you in your home. What an example of Christ!

The Bible maps out a challenging road for each of us, and I have walked mine. I can assure you this is true: suffering produces endurance, which in turn produces character, which produces hope; we can trust that hope and know we won't be put to shame for believing.

This is a grand collaboration, the Bible tells us. That hope is tied up with God's love and poured into our hearts with the help of the Holy Spirit. Despite the challenges of my life, I have grabbed hold of that hope with both hands.

Nobody wants trials and pain. Nobody in her right mind would go out and say, "Please, cause me some pain."

But, since in most cases you can't change what is happening in a painful crisis, you can do the next best thing: take control of how you will handle it. It's an old cliché that God won't give you more than you can handle. But it's my experience that He pushes it sometimes!

Just as I hear the voice of my father in my ears sometimes, encouraging me, our family has had to deal with other voices. Many people, including doctors, have advised us to put Dulci into a facility because it would be "easier" on our family. They don't understand that you don't just throw away a child given to you. She's perfect, and if it takes others a while to realize that, I try to be patient as this is a learning process for them.

Other voices have criticized the size of our family.

Why are you having more children?

Don't you know what causes that?

Why would you bring another child into a home with a father who has cancer? He could die any moment, and then where would you be?

But the fact remains that we *did* get through our trials, and our children helped us with that. They are the ones who have helped me to refrain from concentrating on the negatives, to look instead at the blessings. They are the ones who made me determined to fight on and keep going. They kept me busy and full of laughter and love.

And, of course, the sufferance produced the endurance—and the endurance has been vindicated. We have survived! In particular, the first of us to be ill, Ron, didn't die when any of our children were small or since. In fact, our youngest child is in her last years of high school.

Despite the Bible's teachings about large families being a blessing, even faithful Christians have bought in to the lie that the only socially responsible family is a small one. I wasn't surprised when a new study in 2013 by Ohio State University found that children from larger families are less likely to divorce because they've developed experience with personal relationships that translates into stability later on in their own marriages. One of the researchers talked about the "good effect" of seven or more siblings.

"Growing up in a family with siblings, you develop a set of skills for negotiating both negative and positive interactions," said OSU professor Doug Downey, co-author of the study. "You have to consider other people's points of view, learn how to talk through problems. The more siblings you have, the more opportunities you have to practice those skills." *http://researchnews.osu.edu/archive/sibdivorce.htm*

This might mean that, just as I hear my father's voice in my ear, encouraging me, perhaps the children of large families hear the voices of their brothers and sisters in their ears, telling them to get along. This sort of experience is what the other author of another study, Donna Bobbitt-Zeher, called the source of "additional help in dealing with a marriage relationship as an adult."

Maybe it is the knowledge that while there are more people cheering us on, there are also more people to whom we are accountable. If you have learned the skill of protecting, you would protect your loved ones from your own rashness, wouldn't you?

Personally, I think everyone could benefit from a little fear. I feared my father because I respected him and didn't want to disappoint him. I fear God, too. You can't go through the medical trials we've endured without being sobered by the fact that it is God alone who holds the keys to death. I don't fear God on account of death; death reminds me that I must make the right kinds of decisions in order to attain eternal life.

Without fear you can't have humility. Humility is what makes you put others above yourself. I believe the truth of Proverbs 1:7—the fear of the Lord is the beginning of knowledge.

I still have lessons to learn in this life. I don't want to be the fool whom the writer of Proverbs said despises wisdom and instruction. I want to do everything I can to keep my head and heart clear so that I can always hear the voice of a father, cheering me on, telling me I can do any task that's set before me.

14

THE THREAD THAT TIES OUR SOULS TO THIS LIFE

One of the most valuable gifts we gave our family was the experience of spending summers camping out, four to six weeks at a time. Our favorite place, Triponds Camp Resort in Allegan, Michigan, was the site of some of our most memorable experiences. But it seems as though we never left the excitement of our lives behind; instead, we seemed to attract new crises.

One Sunday the older children had gone on excursions with their friends, and a girlfriend, Donna Byers, and I were walking leisurely along the shore of one of the ponds. It was a peaceful afternoon, and the surface of the water was serene. There little Jordan and Ron was squatting, trying to get his remote control boat to navigate the waters, and we watched and laughed.

Suddenly behind us, off in the distance about 200 yards away, we heard a sharp cry of terror and desperation. "My mom! My mom needs help!" screamed a distraught young woman with two small children in tow.

"I'll go for help," Donna called over her shoulder as she began to run to the manager's house where there was a telephone to call 9-1-1.

Meanwhile, the young woman motioned to us to follow her to a campsite deep in the woods. An older woman with gray hair lay motionless on the ground. Her dentures had fallen out, and a plate of carrots lay strewn all over the ground near the fire pit where she had fallen. She was making strange noises in her throat.

My training in working with the elderly kicked in, and a sense of calm overcame me. I began by carefully tilting back her head and checking her airway for obstructions. Meanwhile the screaming lady was joined by her little children, who began wailing as well. People from all over the camp came running. It seemed as though I were in a tornado, with people moving all around me—the woman on the ground and I at the center of it all.

"You will be okay," I kept telling the woman between breaths as I administered CPR (mouth to mouth resuscitation) and Ron did chest compressions. "Don't worry, the paramedics are coming; you'll be all right."

After a while we heard sirens in the distance, nearly drowned out by the screaming and crying of the poor woman's distraught family. At last the paramedics did come and take over for me. But to everyone's horror the woman died before our eyes as she was being loaded onto the stretcher en route to the ambulance.

"It was a massive heart attack," one of the paramedics said to me, stroking my arm. "You did all you could. There's nothing anyone could have done—even if she'd been in a hospital, they couldn't have saved her." I sat down, hard. Her life had literally been in my hands. And now she was dead. Strangers from all over the camp stood awkwardly, not knowing what to do for the sobbing daughter and grandchildren who clung to one another. I knew the sound of mourning over a loved one. I had heard that sound before, myself, when Joshua died. I knew what it meant to see someone you loved leaving in an ambulance and knowing you would never again see him alive.

But when Joshua died I had a kind of peace, because I knew there was nothing I could do or could have done. With this woman's situation, I had believed I'd arrived in time to make a difference. Yet no matter how hard I had tried, I had failed.

I saw the scene, relived the scene, over and over in my mind for weeks. It was days before I could sleep at night. I could not forget it—will remember it all my life. I wouldn't have believed that with all our family had been through I need to be reminded of how fragile life is, and how precious. But once again, when that woman passed away, I saw the delicate nature of the thread that ties our souls to this life.

Another time we were at the same campground with about twenty of our friends gathered around picnic tables. People were laughing, talking and loading up their plates with food. We had made shish kabobs, and the smell of the charred meat and pungent vegetables drifted over the campground as we gathered to eat. Tired from a long day of activities, Dulci lay napping in our trailer, and several other campers, anxious to get campsites set up, were crowding their trailers into spaces nearby.

One man positioned his trailer closer to ours than we would have done, but since we could see our trailer from where we sat we decided not to make an issue of it. I saw him open the trailer door and go inside, and then, distracted by the conversation over the meal, I looked away.

Suddenly there was a thunderous sound, and smoke was everywhere. Ron and I ran toward our trailer, because from our vantage point it looked as though it was on fire. At that moment the young man we'd seen before emerged from his trailer. His hair was wild and singed and his skin blackened. Worse yet, some of his skin was beginning to peel off. He moaned in pain and began to tremble.

"I think he's going into shock," I told Ron. I motioned to a friend who had run over to get Dulci from our trailer and then turned to Ron.

"Quick—get our water hose and I'll make him sit down."

The man was shaking uncontrollably.

"The water heater . . ." he mumbled. "Tried to light the water heater . . ."

We ran water over his skin to cool it, and whenever we tried take the hose away he would reach for it so we would continue. It seemed like hours that he let the water run over his skin. At last he motioned to us.

"I'd really like a cigarette," he whispered. Ron looked at him for a moment, then reached into his pocket and lit one for the young man. We kept the water flowing over his skin until the emergency personnel came. Our last sight was of this dripping, blackened artichoke of a person putting out a cigarette so he could be loaded into an ambulance. But this one lived, I thought to myself. It wasn't pretty, but he lived.

These two incidents have fixed in my mind some realities that are part of my life. One is that our family is not the only one to suffer tragedy and loss. For each of us, unless we die young, there will be funerals to attend and final good-byes at bedsides. No one escapes the intrusion of death, either for loved ones or for self. And, as the death of the woman reinforced for me, sometimes we are powerless before its force.

I also see a benefit to all of the trials our family has been through. For one thing, I have faced enough crises in my life to have a sense of purpose even in the midst of bad things happening all around me. I can give CPR to a stranger or hose down a burn victim because I've seen the elderly in the nursing homes where I've worked come to their own hours of crisis, and they have trusted me to find help for them. I've been told the worst possible news about my husband, my sons (more to come on this one), my daughter; and that has prepared me, perhaps even numbed me to panic in such situations.

This calmness is not a skill I've developed, or even one that I sought. It is a gift from God, because I have stared death in the face over and over and can do it without blinking because I know the One who always conquers death itself in the end.

I saw that same peace on the face of a newly widowed friend recently at her husband's funeral. Near the casket were pictures of her with her new husband on their long-ago wedding day, both of them full of hope for the future. But while at the present time all around this woman were people weeping and sobbing, she stood tall, in perfect peace and composure. Only God can give a woman who has loved her husband the ability to smile and even to comfort others at his funeral. Only God can give someone the grace to give away her peace and not be the poorer for it.

Another important truth I've learned is that people—all people—need each other. The choking woman needed someone. Her daughter needed someone. The burned man needed someone. The people at the funeral needed someone.

As I look back at the kinds of crises our family has faced, I am humbled by the sheer numbers of people we needed. People to help watch our children while we ministered to the one who was hurting most. People who prepared meals and ran errands. People who sat at bedsides of loved ones in the hospital when we could not.

People who did things out of any normal comfort zone, like handling bedpans or cleaning up messes. These were people who gave us comfort when we had no bright plans for the future, who gave us help when we were literally helpless.

Of course, our extended family has done more for us than we could ever repay or even recount. And we've been borne along by the large and small acts of kindness from doctors, nurses, therapists and strangers. It's certainly true that God is the source of all help, but sometimes I feel like the little boy whose mother assured him at bedtime that angels would guard him as he slept.

"But I need someone with skin on," he objected. In our times of trial we too needed someone with skin on, and God has always provided just the person, just the skills, and just in time.

15

MENTORS AND MUSIC

I know that no one who reads of my experiences will say "I'd really like to be tested like that." No one in his right mind would seek to be at the hub of such a revolving wheel of illnesses and distress.

But I have learned a sad fact about my faith: I am spiritually strongest when I am in the valleys of my life. That's when I feel closest to God—when I am on my knees, earnestly talking to Him. That's when I feel His comfort and His arms wrapped around my sagging shoulders.

On the other hand, when everything is going well, I feel that I am capable of handling things. "I can do this," I say to myself. "I'm all right now." He's still there in my life, but I'm sorry to say that when I hold Him at a distance I begin to feel that He isn't so close to me.

I'm glad to say that He doesn't let me get too far away! Sometimes He is that ringing voice in my head, getting my attention when I'm not listening. He tells me what is right and what is wrong. He tells me He can work through me, even when I am in a valley.

"Remember that situations are not about you," my mother always reminds me, and I know that this is counsel from the Lord. Even though I may feel I am the hub of events and even tragedies that are swirling around, my mother reminds me that if I am at the center it is so that other people can be encouraged by observing my Christian walk—to see how I am handling difficulties. That gives me the perspective to move some of my focus away from myself and to think about how, at any given moment, the faith of other people may be growing not through their own personal trials but through mine.

That makes me very humble and reminds me that I have an obligation from God to tell people what has helped me through difficult times—factors such as laughter and music and Scriptures and faith. I also have to plainly say why it is that I can endure and triumph in difficulties. This is not my personal strength. (You can't rely on that when you can't even toilet yourself, as I couldn't after the automobile accident.)

It can't be just the possession of a sunny disposition. There is something under my smile, and it is my peace with God. He and I don't fight. When I can think clearly I cooperate with Him, because He's got the perfect game plan. But we live at peace with one another even when I don't understand why things happen as they do.

So what would people want to know about how to handle repeated and grievous trials? Can I counsel them to have a cheerful disposition, when I know that mine was a gift from God that didn't come with a cut-and-paste function to pass along intact to others? Can I tell them "Just trust God" as I do? Well, yes—given that the trust is built on some kind of solid knowledge of who God is.

I feel great compassion for other parents who have lost children, for other families struck with incurable illnesses and intractable situations. I can understand why such people might succumb to the bitterness of their tragedies and assume that God doesn't love them or that He was punishing them in some way. Believe me, I get it. But we can't use our own life experiences to make judgments about God. Those feelings and conclusions can change with every circumstance.

The reality is that *He* doesn't change. And He doesn't back off from what He's told us about His character. We have to base what we know about Him on what He says about Himself, because He is incapable of lying.

I was involved in a group Bible study at the time the accident occurred that took Joshua's life. Before that event I had sometimes participated as a leader. Part of the preparation for each week's study involved my meeting with mentors, women in my congregation I admired; and with accountability partners who helped me grow in the Word. These wonderful women never maintained an enforced distance between themselves and me—some of them even volunteered to watch my children while I attended leadership training. One of them brought my infant Jordan to me during lunch so I could nurse him while I learned more about God, about His Word, and about how to teach it to others more effectively.

As a mother of four young children, I knew I had a lot to learn, and the course of study had been the four Gospels. We had just begun the book of Acts (referred to in some translations as the Acts of the Apostles) when we suffered that horrendous automobile accident. Afterward these mentors became even more diligent servants to me, truly exemplifying the care of the first-century church of Acts. (Maybe we could call the many ways in which they helped me with my home and my children the Acts of the Mentors.)

A young people's group at our church provided Bible instruction for Ron and me early on in our marriage, and we have grown and aged together as a group through many years. During this time we have together conducted straight Bible studies, watched Rob Bell videos and Ray Vanderlaan lessons from Israel, and participated in various studies on parenting.

There has been a rhythm of service in this group. When one couple was doing well they would help someone else facing a trial or a valley, with food, flowers, fellowship and steady friendship. Those who were serving during a time of calm in their lives would invariably down the road become recipients of the group's love as a trial would befall them.

Trials come to us all, sooner or later. Jesus was quite the realist when He flatly told His disciples that "in this world you will have trouble." I can imagine them sitting there thinking, as I did when I was first married, that trouble was for other people. Or that if Ron and I were going to have trouble, it would be when we were old. Not right away.

In our close-knit little church group we have faced the deaths of brothers, mothers, fathers; rejoiced over weddings; commiserated about broken ankles and lost jobs and cancer. This group has made it possible for us never to feel that we are in a valley alone. In fact, I don't know how anyone gets through a life full of trials without a support group of fellow believers.

In addition, for the last five years I've participated with other women in two Bible studies I really love. One I began with my friend Kay when we dreamed of an environment where we could share "woman time," friendship and Bible study all at the same time. We used Francine Rivers's *A Lineage of Grace*, which encouraged us as we observed some of the most scandal-challenged women of the Bible—Tamar, Rahab, Ruth, Bathsheba and Mary— rise above their circumstances. If God chose them, honored their faith and showed His glory through them, just think what *we* could do!

Now I'm in a Bible study with author Lynnelle Pierce, who meets with fifty or so local women to examine what the Bible says about the Holy Spirit. I can't wait for Monday nights to meet with those women and pray and study the Bible. It's the highlight of my week.

Another thing that has helped me through my whole life is the role of music. When I was a child my family always had music playing—the music of Lawrence Welk, "HeeHaw" and Green Valley Jamboree. My Mom loved country singers like George Jones and Johnny Cash, while my father favored Duke Ellington and Frank Sinatra. Both of them loved hymns, both listening to and singing them.

One of my earliest memories is of my grandmother pushing me in an old tire swing, singing of the sad fate of the Babes in the Wood and the faithfulness of Old Shep— sad songs that would bring us all to tears. We recorded both songs, so that grandchildren to come will be able to hear her voice and share in that part of their heritage from her.

She encouraged her daughter, my mother, then still a child, to sing in front of her church, which she did beautifully. But Grandma had to give her a handkerchief to hold on to so she wouldn't be overcome by shyness and pull her skirt up over her face.

Music was an essential part of our road trips too; I can still hear my father's voice booming out all the old songs, like "There Was an Old Lady Who Swallowed a Fly," "Joshua Fought the Battle of Jericho," and "You Are My Sunshine."

By the time I became a teenager, disco music filled our home, and I've made it part of my home too. My children have danced joyfully, Misty and Belle enjoying line dancing and more formal dance classes since they were little.

Our home has never been a place of solemnity and suffering, and now our children's lives are filled with music and performance. Jordan has taught line dancing and plays the guitar, DeeDee has sung in choir and a music group for her school, and all of the children played some sort of instrument in school—Misty and her saxophone, DeeDee and her cornet, Jordan with his trombone, Belle with her clarinet, and Sadie with her flute and vocal performances. Our house was often the embodiment of a joyful noise!

I have a roster of favorite songs that encourage and uplift me. They include "Holy, Holy, Holy"; "Ten Thousand Angels"; "Lead Me, Guide Me"; "His Eye Is on the Sparrow"; "One Day at a Time"; "Amazing Grace"; and "How Great Thou Art."

Ron loves all kinds of music, especially Christian music. His favorites are "My Tribute" and "Amazing Grace." He also loves to laugh along with some of his beloved Christian comedians, including Mark Lowry, Dennis Swanberg, Ken Davis and Mike Warnke. And to this day our children's lives are being blessed by Casting Crowns, MercyMe, Matthew West, Chris Tomlin, Hillsong, Matt Redman, David Crowder, and the Newsboys.

For ten years Ron and I attended the Gaither Praise Gathering in Indianapolis. There our souls were fed with songs, uplifting comedy, and testimonies of how other people overcame their lives' obstacles.

We took the Scriptural commandments to sing and make music in our hearts very seriously, and this has blessed us beyond measure. Each of our children would tell you that hidden in their hearts are the great hymns that have been part of their entire lives.

I've often said that one way I've gotten through our trials is by refusing to think too deeply about them.

Instead I concentrate on what I know to be true. Bible study has been a make-it-or-break it necessity in my life, and music carries me along over the roughest waves.

In fact, I could say that music and dancing and laughter have saved all our souls. Some of my fondest memories are of my children gathered in our living room, twirling and swirling to music, collapsing with laughter at their own mistakes, singing along at the tops of their lungs with songs that brought them joy in the midst of circumstances that would have kept others in tears.

16

READING LIPS

When you are in the middle of a trial, there is always a sense that if you can just get through it things will go back to some sort of normalcy. I think I had that hope when Ron began having his first medical problems, early in our marriage. Once we got the diagnosis and were set up for surgery, I believed we would just have our baby and go back to our former life, enhanced, of course, by the new addition to our family.

However, once Joshua was born, Ron's problems weren't all over. Yet with each new occurrence of cancer or discovery of another condition, in the back of my mind was the thought that we'd all be sitting around saying "Whew, that was a close one!" and that then our lives would resume.

The Bible portrays the growth of faith, beginning when the seeds of God's promises to bless us and do good for us are planted in our minds. I learned of God and His goodness in Sunday School, from my parents, and from songs and Scriptures. I grew up with an absolute confidence that God loved me, that He wanted the best for me, and that He would always be with me. I carried those assurances with me as I went through high school, began my jobs and other training, and especially when I entered into marriage.

But all true faith is tested when your real life problems slam right into those promises, and neither one will budge. I knew that God loved me and loved my children. Yet one of those children did not survive a horrible wreck that left his father and me with lifelong effects. I knew God's promises to believers who love Him that He would bring good from all circumstances. But look at the circumstances we have had!

I trusted God with my marriage, my health, my children. But each of these was threatened—actually menaced—by events and circumstances that made our blood run cold and tested us to the limits of our endurance.

Of course my faith—and this, often in open warfare against my sight—told me that God would keep those promises. And indeed He has. He has brought good out of every bad circumstance we have experienced. Sometimes I have had to just hold on and believe there *would be* a time when He would make His purposes clearer, would bring the blessings of the sun after the thunderstorm.

I have also learned that God doesn't perform this sequence for us in neat little packages. He doesn't necessarily wait for the resolution of one situation before He puts us right back into a different pot of hot water. Sometimes the phases of situations seem to overlap like shingles; you can't see the ending of one before the beginning of another. But, like shingles protecting a roof, the whole process, and the assurance of God that He'll be with us despite the seeming contradictions, becomes a shielding protection for us as we trust Him and look at His track record of resolving our troubles.

That was the case with our beautiful little daughter Misty. Before the death of Joshua, when Misty was eighteen months old, she had a fever of 105 degrees. We weren't aware at first that the fever had affected her ears so severely that she had lost much of her hearing. She was such a quiet and shy girl that it wasn't noticeable. In addition, she was very clever at masking her hearing loss and learning to read lips on her own.

But I had suspicions. This compliant little girl, who would burst into tears if she even thought her parents were displeased with her, would not answer us when her back was turned. Her voice had an odd monotone quality to it. But it was hard to believe she couldn't hear because she functioned in almost all situations as though she could. She was so good at this that when she was four years old and I finally determined there was a problem, even doctors were skeptical.

"You're just an overprotective mom," the first ear, nose, and throat specialist assured me. They made me feel guilty for still letting her use a pacifier at age three. "You're just imagining things."

A second audiologist said he could find nothing wrong with Misty's hearing. So did a third. But I am a momma bear when it comes to my children. If I know there is something wrong, I will fight for them. I won't rest until I find out.

At last a new audiologist did an extensive hearing test and confirmed my fears. More than sixty percent of Misty's hearing was gone. But there was a solution, and thank God she was able to use hearing aids. Once she had her hearing aids, her ability was boosted to ninety percent. I knew it. I knew it.

By then she had developed such incredible compensating skills with lip reading that the person making the molds for her ears soon learned that she had to cover her mouth with her hand if she didn't want Misty to just read her lips when she was assessing her.

The horrific events that led to Joshua's death in the car accident and the hospitalization and long recovery for Ron and me happened just as Misty was being fitted for her hearing aids and getting started at a new preschool. While we were struggling quite literally with staying alive and with the agony of losing one child, another precious child was being lovingly cared for when we ourselves could do nothing for her.

A new teacher understood how disorienting it could be for a preschool child to suddenly hear raucous sounds in a world that previously had offered only soft, muffled tones. She comforted Misty and helped her to adjust. Another teacher would take her from class and give her special training, and yet another's interactions with Misty made the shy little girl feel loved and secure.

But many struggles lay ahead for Misty. The challenges of living in a world of noise interfered with her ability to learn to read—something her teachers did not tell me until the end of the second grade. But we spent a summer and the entire next year catching her up to her classmates' reading skills.

Like many children, Misty did not want other children to know about her disability. She would keep her ears covered by her hair and never talked about her difficulty with hearing. Inevitably there was teasing, as from a boy on her bus who asked her, "Are you from hearing aid kingdom?" She worried that others would see her as different and would not want to spend time with her.

"If someone just cares about your hearing aid, they're not your friend!" I would tell her.

Some activities were difficult for her, such as swimming. For one thing, she couldn't wear her hearing aids in the water so she was often unaware of people speaking to her. And what does a preteenager do with hearing aids when they're not being used? How safe is anyplace poolside? Nonetheless, she was very conscientious with her hearing aids, wearing them even though she didn't really want to. She kept close tabs on where they were and learned the hard way that a hearing aid dropped onto the floor could become a dog's snack.

Despite her hearing loss, she soared in her achievement in anything she wanted to do. She played soccer and volleyball, performed Dutch dance routines, and worked at a retirement home for ten years—where she could offer true empathy to older people who were losing their hearing, too. She made her way successfully through high school, Calvin College, and the University of Michigan, where she got her master's degree in social work, specializing in geriatrics. She has definitely overcome any obstacle that her hearing might have posed.

It took a long time, up until college, for her to be less self-conscious about her hearing. Long before she was able to disregard her hearing aids, though, her friends came to see them as a "nonissue." And when she met the young man who would later become her husband, he told her they were "sexy."

And that settled that.

17

No Mistakes

Although Misty wouldn't think of herself as a trailblazer, her hearing problems—and the difficulty I had in getting them diagnosed—certainly made it easier when our young son Jordan lost much of his hearing when he was four years old. The tubes that were supposed to control the chronic problem of fluid in his ears didn't make any difference. He still had a forty percent hearing loss.

This time—perhaps because of hard-won credibility from advocating for Misty—I had no difficulty getting a diagnosis and assessment, and Jordan began wearing his hearing aids at age five. But because he was a rough-and-tumble boy, his hearing aids didn't always stay in his ears. For one thing, they weren't as easy to hide as long-haired Misty's had been, and he was reluctant to wear them when he was teased by classmates. More than one schoolyard fight, I know, started with an insult about his hearing aids.

They went from his ears into his pockets and then into the washing machine. Or they ended up in strange places. Many times we searched on hands and knees the living room, his bedroom, and even the garbage and sandbox for lost hearing aids. Thank goodness for Children's Special Health Care Services, which covered the $3,000 cost of each aid when they weren't recovered.

Jordan's hearing loss prevented him from starting school with other children his age, and he began preschool at age six. The aides at his school also made special arrangements to keep his scholastic progress in step with that of his peers. Even more, the school installed carpets to cut down on ambient noise and put tennis balls on the bottoms of chair legs to reduce the scraping sounds they made. One teacher even wore a microphone that broadcast directly to Jordan's hearing aids. As he grew the devices became less annoying to him. He, too, learned to overcome the limitations of hearing loss, and like his sister Misty he has been successful.

Still, having two children with hearing loss was discouraging to me. When it was diagnosed, I had a sinking feeling. I began counting off on my fingers. Every one of my six surviving children had a problem of some sort.

"Why can't these children be perfect?" I asked God. "Isn't that what every parent wants for all their children? Why at such a young age do they have to struggle with such things?"

In the case of Misty and Jordan, I knew that hearing loss usually doesn't get "cured." After the diagnosis and even with technological advances, I knew that our children would face difficulties of varying degrees for the rest of their lives, not just while they lived in our home. I pray that the percentage of hearing that Misty and Jordan have will not decrease. The possibility of that troubles me greatly.

Hearing loss isn't a challenge just for a child; it can be very frustrating for a parent. Repeating, repeating, repeating instructions. Not being heard and, in some cases, a parent not being able to understand.

In adulthood people can compensate and work around obstacles to hearing, but some issues that other people might never consider are ever present factors. There's the inconvenience and expense of the aids and, of course, of the batteries, which always seem to fail at an inopportune time. When a hearing aid isn't working, often the wearer doesn't notice the silence and can miss out on important sounds.

Crowded places and restaurants are often filled with harsh noises, and having to say "What?" all the time is frustrating for everyone. Outside, wind blowing in your ear can cancel out other sounds. And then there's the embarrassing whistle the little devices can make. But still, without God's intervention hearing loss will have to be a consideration in every element of their lives until the time God heals these children of mine in heaven. Why, I ask, has God allowed me the pleasure of two children who happen to have hearing loss?

God makes no mistakes. His ways aren't ours. He gives us what we need, not necessarily what we want much of the time. But because of our challenges we are stronger. And we certainly are more humble.

Our children learned early on about what is important and what is not. Misty and Jordan are soft-spoken and have gentle, quiet spirits. They are wonderful listeners—which is the way the Bibles tells us we are all supposed to be, listening more than we speak.

Both are deep, reflective thinkers. Bearing thorns in their flesh, they grew up into a world to which they knew they must accommodate themselves, that would not change for them. They have always been far more mature than others of their chronological ages.

Kids today might say they have special "super powers"—the ability to understand spoken words when no one else can hear them, to "hear" voices talking to them across a crowded room, to communicate with each other accurately and silently. They share a bond that hearing people cannot know.

"Why couldn't my children be perfect?" I asked God again.

And then I looked at myself and Ron. I'm certainly far from perfect, with a smashed-in nose that embarrasses me and lingering physical limitations from the accident, surgeries, and illnesses. Like little Dulci and daughter Mercedes, I have developed a curvature of the spine; and thus we three, like Misty and Jordan, are knit together in a troubling and limiting physical condition.

And Ron—he had dealt with slowly progressive hearing loss since his childhood. The slow-growing tumor in his brain, there since birth, robbed him of his hearing bit by bit as he grew up, so slowly that he was reluctant to believe he had a serious problem. It was only after we got married and I could see the troubling progression that I insisted he see a doctor.

If it had not been for his hearing loss, Ron's brain tumor may have continued growing. God used this hearing loss to alert us to a problem and to prevent something much worse. That's the way God works, bringing good even out of bad situations, just as He has promised in Romans 8:28—Ron's favorite verse, his "go-to" Scripture.

Would I have chosen the physical challenges that we as a family and as individuals have faced? Certainly not. Each one felt like a punch in the stomach. In each case my initial reaction was disappointment and sadness.

As a mom I wanted to fix each condition. But as I watched my precious children in their struggles, I recognized that they were under God's protection. They are so resilient. They grow and progress and learn—and overcome. And as I see them joyful and surmounting obstacles, it gives me great joy and peace. "God knows what he is doing, and I need to trust him," I tell myself.

I am not one to search the Internet, researching conditions with which I am unfamiliar. I do not look up the causes of illnesses, the side effects, treatments, or prognoses. This information is not helpful to me because I know God already has a plan. And while I appreciate hearing personal stories of others and how they dealt with trials and treasure the newly-forged relationships with those who share similar stories because they somehow "get it," this is not where I search for answers on what to do. I myself rely on faith alone. No self-help books, no research study, no information from the Internet. I rely on Scripture verses I learned as a child and Scripture verses I leaned on while I was going through a previous trials. God lays these scriptures on my heart at exactly the right time, exactly when I need it.

Whenever I've needed answers, I found that what I already had was enough and more than enough. If there was a need for action I took action. But with things I cannot change I move on. I trust that God will sustain me through the trial as He has so many times, and I lay my head on His chest and rest.

After the initial shock of a new diagnosis or seemingly unbearable news, God gives me this unexplainable sense of peace, something I struggle to describe. Once I have this peace, this special gift, I am able to fully trust Him, giving Him all the glory. This peace allows me to focus on Him rather than focusing on myself, my pain, my fears.

That peaceful security of trust in God would be put to the test once again with yet another of our children. Our only remaining son, Jordan, would soon be fighting, not simply for his hearing, but for his life.

Part Three

A Son's Journey

18

AGGRESSIVE TREATMENT

A few hours of observing our second son, Jordan, would have confirmed to any observer that he was a rowdy little boy. We lost count of the number of scrapes and broken bones he had, but he always—and often quite literally—bounced back.

But after Christmas of 2002 and a bout the next month with a virus, our young teen's strength and energy levels seemed to be flagging. Tests for mononucleosis showed no sign of that illness, but he developed pneumonia in May. His sports physical in April had not shown anything abnormal, but his hemoglobin levels were steadily declining.

The doctor wanted to analyze his blood and urine, but a mother doesn't need tests to know that her son is ill. I could press my finger into the flesh in his legs and the depression would stay, deep and ominous. Jordan and I left the doctor's office, sobered, and went to do the blood work.

His eyes were drowsy all the way home, and I worried as I drove. He went straight to bed, and my suspicions were confirmed when a call from the doctor instructed us to go directly to the hospital for a kidney biopsy. The pediatrician thought our Jordan, age thirteen, had IgA nephropathy, a form of kidney disease marked by protein in the urine and by damage to the kidneys.

We packed hurriedly, and he and I arrived at the hospital after nine p.m. The next hours were a flurry of check-ins, tests and frighteningly high blood pressure readings. Jordan dozed between interruptions, eating a chicken sandwich at three a.m. when he awakened. By morning he was ravenously hungry, eating eggs, French toast and muffins and drinking milk.

After an ultrasound he was excited to learn that members of the Detroit Lions football team were scheduled to pay a visit to the hospital. Maybe this wouldn't be so bad, he said. But his blood pressure kept climbing; so high, in fact, that he had to be transported by ambulance to Ann Arbor to a pediatric kidney doctor.

He missed his opportunity to see his heroes, the Lions, and was greatly disappointed. But he had no idea how much more difficult our lives were about to become, and not just because of his illness. I learned that VERY day that our insurance had been cancelled. Why? Because my husband had been laid off at work. I felt the stress rising within me. No work. No insurance. And most immediate of all—no ambulance without insurance; in fact, no *hospital* for Jordan without insurance.

I called my mother, in tears. And as my mother always does, she handled it. She dispatched our daughter Misty with a check to our insurance agency and then called Children's Special Health Care Services, which put us onto COBRA insurance—but with no grace period.

I began the two-and-a-half hour ambulance ride, frightened by the uncertainty of the situation. I sat in the front of the ambulance, with an emotionless Jordan in the back. During the whole ride he helped the paramedics with his own IVs, medications and blood pressure checks. They worried because his blood pressure was about 200/100.

I could hear the paramedics talk to him about dogs and guns and rabbits and groundhogs and how many times he'd broken his arms. This was a child who'd had stitches in his knee from falling on a seashell on the beach, who'd broken a wrist in basketball and a wrist snow skiing. He'd had loosened teeth and a lip cut wide open from being elbowed in the mouth during basketball practice. He'd even had several concussions from playing football and baseball. Surely, we reasoned, kidney problems couldn't be all that bad.

Even our arrival at the hospital involved mix-ups: being unloaded at the wrong door and then having to load the gurney back up for a ride around the building. The ambulance drivers, who had become our comfort, then left, and I found myself alone.

I cried as I filled out all the forms put in front of me. My son needed surgery, I hadn't eaten all day or slept, and it was three-fifteen in the morning, I knew nobody, and no one was there with me. I could hardly bear it.

Finally, as Jordan left for the biopsy at five a.m., I heard welcome voices. Ron, my mom, and my sister-in-law had come to keep me company. I cried again, but this time with relief and joy. As the morning wore on I called to check on our other children. Misty was bowling with friends and DeeDee was watching the other kids play outside. Life seemed normal. And, we told each other, we would soon have some answers about Jordan.

Except that we didn't. The biopsy was postponed until the next day. I walked my loved ones out to their car to get the change of clothes and camera they'd brought for me. At eight-thirty I stood waving goodbye to them in the dark parking lot, alone again. And locked out of the hospital. Far from any readily accessible entrance, I began to feel desperate. A call on an emergency phone directed me to an elevator—which was locked. Another woman walking through the parking lot had no answers. I was beyond tired, worried sick about my son, and not even able to get into the hospital.

And then a man appeared out of nowhere. He opened the doors with an access card and told me he would be praying for our son. Was he an angel? He surely felt like one. This was a time when God's Word that I had "hidden in my heart," as the psalmist put it, allowed me to press on and to recognize this angel as a messenger of God, assuring me and reminding me that God is always there, *always* watching over me.

The biopsy the next day showed Jordan's kidneys to be enlarged. I wasn't sure what that meant and was just beginning to relax a bit when I saw a doctor come through the door; I could tell from his expression that his news wasn't good. The kidneys, he said, were abnormally pale; a later pathology report indicated that they were scarred and not working properly.

"This will take aggressive treatment," the doctor said.

"What does that mean?"

"Steroids may be able to stop the scarring and other damage to the kidneys."

I sat in silence as the doctor outlined the wide-ranging nature of the treatments Jordan needed: the doses of *more than one hundred pills a day* that he would have to take for high blood pressure, potassium, cholesterol, spilling protein and enzymes into the urine. This along with iron injections to increase his red blood cells and blood count tests twice a week.

I wanted what every mother would have wanted at that moment: to get into the hospital bed, take his treatments for him, and let him go home and be a little boy again—something the coming days would never again permit.

I tried to keep him occupied with movies and games from the hospital's activity room. But often there wasn't much time for entertainment. His life became very busy—rarely did we get to bed until before one a.m. because of all the tests, procedures, weight checks, examinations and medications he required.

The pills were the most daunting. He could take only one at a time—and then, sometimes only if crushed. The hospital food was, well—hospital food. Sometimes the highlight of his day was something from the fast-food restaurant in the hospital. It became an adventure to go there—his IV would allow only half an hour before sounding an alarm when disconnected. Once Jordan impressed his fellow diners by expertly turning off the alarm. But he apparently pulled too hard on the needle, and back in the room the adhesive tape had to be removed, causing the worst and most annoying pain. Tests, more tests, more treatments, more medications.

"His kidneys are only functioning at about 25 percent," a doctor told us a few days later. "Eventually he will need dialysis."

I absorbed this. The doctor hesitated before he finished.

"And a transplant. There's no way around that."

I shook my head, trying to absorb what that meant. The doctor went on to explain that Jordan could go home eventually but that I would be trained to give him his medications and injections, to take his blood pressure and carefully monitor his weight, and to use a stethoscope and all the other devices that would be necessary. Next a nutritionist came in to explain what a diet low in sodium and phosphate would look like. I learned how to give Jordan his shots: wiping off the back of his arm, pinching the skin, putting the needle in quickly but injecting and withdrawing it slowly. "It didn't hurt . . . that much," Jordan affirmed, valiantly, after the first time. I don't know who was more scared, he or I.

Our lives had changed—again. Of course all of this meant I couldn't go back to work—at least not right away. But when I phoned into my job where I worked as a cosmetologist, a fellow employee refused to make some calls to clients for me, to cancel appointments.

"I can't do your work for you," she pointed out.

I was stunned, still reeling from my new "job" description, and this felt like hitting a brick wall. Jordan's medical problems, though overwhelming in their own way, didn't feel "personal." But this certainly did. I felt sad and numb.

My life in the hospital with Jordan took on a kind of crazy tempo that would go on for a couple of weeks more. Bible study, endless tests and procedures for Jordan, walks, trips to the activity room, increasing boredom in between for us both. At night my mind would spin with questions.

Here again, although I felt my family "home" was being knocked to the ground again one brick at a time, I knew that the foundation wouldn't fail. Instead of being frustrated by my inability to get to sleep, I knew the Lord wanted fellowship with me during those quiet times. I knew I should be listening, and soon I got the message: be still and know that I am God. I didn't know our future, but I knew *Who* was in charge of it.

As the days progressed I learned more about Jordan's disease. Most cases of IgA nephropathy are incurable. It's caused by deposits of the protein immunoglobulin A (IgA), called glomeruli, into the filters of the kidneys. Jordan's filters had stopped their normal job of sending wastes and excess water from the blood to become urine and flow down to the bladder. Instead, blood waste products were not removed and protein spilled into the urine, accompanied by swelling in the hands and feet. The worsening process could continue for ten or twenty years.

End-stage renal disease meant dialysis and perhaps a transplant. The words "end-stage" filled me with fear. That's where we were. But friends and family members sometimes made the three-hour trip to the hospital to encourage us, bring us gifts and food, and to pray with us. At home Misty and DeeDee held down the family fort in innumerable areas of service.

One day as we sat in the hospital courtyard with family, I felt as though perhaps life could get back to normal. The fresh air, the view of the sky, the plants and the quiet atmosphere reminded me that there was a real world of beauty and peace outside the walls.

But by the time we returned to Jordan's room and learned that the staff had been looking for us, I knew more bad news was coming. The doctor's voice was flat.

"Jordan's kidneys are worse," she said. "He is retaining more and more fluid. We'll have to start the dialysis right away."

I described the feeling later as like being hit in the head with a baseball bat. I sat in total silence. I couldn't cry. I couldn't speak. But once again a supernatural event happened. A peace, warm as a blanket on a cold evening, began to wrap itself around me. What had earlier been just the absence of emotion was replaced by the presence of something that calmed and strengthened me.

I looked up at the doctor, wondering what she must be thinking of my reaction—or rather, my lack of reaction. Did she think I didn't care? I felt a slight pang of guilt for not crying. But the peace was so complete that I could only sit quietly in the chair.

"I feel so bad that this isn't getting any better," she finally said. She arose and left the little conference room where we'd met and went to share the news with Jordan and my mother and sister-in-law.

The activity level around Jordan accelerated. Preparations began for dialysis ports to be inserted into his stomach and chest. He would stay in the hospital for two more weeks and go onto a kidney transplant list.

Our schedule, if it could be called that, seemed frantic and upside-down. Jordan couldn't sleep at night and dozed during the day between the visits by doctors and other healthcare providers. We often stayed up and watched "Whose Line Is It Anyway?" and "Walker, Texas Ranger" to pass the time, and sometimes scurried around the hospital hallways, playing spies and cops and robbers. I realized that one reason God had given me to him as a mother is that I require very little sleep and was able to keep him company during the dark watches.

The night before his surgery was one of those. Jordan had a bad stomachache and lay in my lap until an injection eased the pain. The surgery to insert the ports and a neck catheter went well, but when Jordan came out he was in pain, and his body was swollen. He went immediately to dialysis. At his side I sat and watched my son's blood coming out of his body and returning mysteriously clean.

The next day, though, the swelling was back. Another round of dialysis took away the swelling, as well as helping his vaulting blood pressure to stabilize. Soon we settled into that new rhythm of dangerous levels and then temporary relief as his blood was cleansed.

Along the way God provided for me, as He always has, with opportunities to minister to others. I became a trusty tour guide for new patients' families who were as confused as I'd been about the hospital's layout. In another instance friends came to the hospital with a daughter who had a suspicious growth on her knee that needed to be removed. I was happy to make them feel welcome and oriented in a place that had been my home for a month.

A couple of days into this process Ron called with more distressing news: his father's heart valve had failed, and the family had gathered to say their final goodbyes. As I so often had, I felt the tug of divided responsibilities. I wanted to be in two places at once. But God's wisdom had brought all of his brothers and sisters to our area a few days earlier for a family reunion and camping trip that had been planned for months, so Ron had the comfort of loved ones close by during this difficult time. Ron's father passed away the same day that Jordan was released from the hospital.

Back at home our lives settled into a new rhythm that would be repeated hundreds of times in trips from our home for dialysis three hours away in Ann Arbor. Sometimes we tried to break up the schedule, but with varying degrees of success: a camping trip to nearby lakes became a nightmare when the peritoneal dialysis he had been on for a year failed on our trip. At home some nights were filled with the nerve-wracking sounds of the machine's warning bells and alerts when it malfunctioned.

One day the phone rang; it was a woman from church. "Look, we know that your medical bills must be overwhelming," she said kindly. "Our company, Pennzoil Oil Change, would like to help with money for travel and medical for you." I was so grateful because the doctors required that we stay nearby in a hotel in Ann Arbor for the first few sessions of peritoneal dialysis. It was a great relief to have that paid for.

Jordan and I treated our dialysis trips as a kind of adventure. One time Jordan's football coach, Walter Lamb, arranged for us to attend a University of Michigan football game and meet the coach and players, who gave

Jordan an autographed football. I hesitate to say that our trips back and forth were fun—but we did enjoy looking for deer on the road, talking and joking. We had begun to accept our "new reality" and make the best of it. Jordan never complained and never cried, no matter how much the many procedures must have hurt.

A local television news program broadcast a story about the fundraiser. It was sobering to me—I saw our situation for the first time through the eyes of others. Jordan did not have a bright future, it seemed. But he had the brilliance of his own serenity. And he was surrounded by people who loved him and were glad to sacrifice for him.

And in a way that still causes wonder in my heart, Jordan's suffering was not only an inspiration to others; it may have saved my life.

19

RESCUED AGAIN

One of the recurrent problems that plagued Jordan's dialysis treatments was difficulty with the peritoneal dialysis catheter in his abdomen. Finally the doctors surgically removed his omentum, the apron-like sheet of fatty tissue that covers the large intestine, and his dialysis went much more smoothly from that point forward. In fact, his kidneys began to regain some function to the point that he was able to stop dialysis for almost two years. No doctor had expected this.

This "breather" was an incredible blessing because being on a kidney transplant list required a minimum of three years. And so, thanks be to God, two of those were free from the pain and travel and inconvenience of dialysis. This was actually a time of many blessings. First, during that time a pediatric dialysis unit opened in nearby Grand Rapids. Second, during that two years Jordan got his driver's license and was able to drive himself to appointments. Ah! Sweet freedom for us both!

I would have to remind myself when I looked at my happy family that one of us had a terminal illness that could eventually cost him his kidneys or perhaps his life. Once again I felt the gift God had given me: a disposition that sees the sun behind the clouds, the blessings in the tragedy, the hand of God holding me up. I am a "fixer" who wants to make everything all right for my loved ones, but after God lets me try—lets me participate—He reminds me that He and He alone is in control.

That knowledge would be very important in the middle of Jordan's trials when I went in for tests to see whether one of my kidneys might be a suitable match for him. I can help fix it, I thought.

Imagine my shock when the blood tests revealed that I, too, needed to be fixed. For more than fifteen years, since the automobile accident that had cost Joshua his life and had kept me under medical care for the two following years, my body had been harboring a secret. The blood transfusion I'd received just after the accident had given me Hepatitis C.

My first reaction was of horror. Hepatitis C is a serious illness. From being around ill people in nursing homes I knew what was coming, and it was worse than I thought. The treatment was six months of antiviral interferon injections that I had to administer to myself in the leg or the stomach. The first shot was done under a doctor's supervision. I had given shots to others. How hard could all this be? "This is a piece of cake," I told myself, congratulating myself on the ease of the injection.

I went out to eat with a girlfriend and then to the Parade of Homes. Within a few hours I began shaking with chills, and only piles of blankets at home and ibuprofen took care of the fever. But that reaction set up a fearful and recurrent scenario for me, and only daily calls from our daughter Misty at college got me through it.

"You can do it, Mom," she would say over the phone. "One, two, three, go!"—and then I would give myself the chemo shots. My skin took on a pale tinge of green, I sometimes fainted, and I lost about fifteen pounds during those six months. Still, with Misty's help I got through it. Subsequent blood tests showed that the hepatitis was gone.

But for me that crisis wasn't the most significant aspect of having Hepatitis C. The disease destroys the liver, slowly and silently, over the course of about thirty years. I would never have known to be tested unless my son's illness had required a kidney transplant. Ironically, through the course of his suffering I was healed. As Jordan would say, "I got kidney failure to save you, Mom."

But unfortunately, Jordan's "breather" days of health were coming to an end. We didn't know it then, but the two years that had been such a gift of God to our weary souls were up. Once again his blood pressure shot up. His kidneys were tired. They were finished.

This time when he entered the hospital it wasn't with a frantic, lonely mother. An entire choir of thirty young people crowded into his room to sing and pray for him—and in the case of one over-emotional young girl, to faint for him. His sister Misty started an internet "caring" page for friends to receive updates about his progress.

A new port was inserted into his chest so that he could restart hemodialysis at the hospital. Additional tests showed that his kidney function had dropped to fifteen percent. He went in for dialysis three times a week and settled in waiting for a new kidney.

His sister DeeDee, just as I had, underwent tests to see whether she could be an organ donor for him. The two small kidney stones discovered in the testing process wouldn't prevent her from donating.

"Let's wait through the Christmas season," one of the doctors told us. "If there's not a donor, we'll look at DeeDee."

I nodded. We had airline tickets and our passports ready for a holiday vacation to Mexico, and I told the doctor about the proposed trip.

"Oh, don't go anywhere. If your son is going to get a donated kidney from outside the family, Christmas is the best time."

I must have looked puzzled, so he explained. "Winter, especially during the Christmas season, is a time of depression for many people, and they take their lives." I sat staring until the truth dawned on me. Jordan's life depended on someone else's death. And we would have to be ready at any moment to put aside our holiday celebration not only for a surgery but for sadness for the loss another family would cry over; for gratitude toward someone we could never thank.

On December 31, 2006, when Jordan was seventeen years old, we returned home from church and saw Jordan with a packed bag.

"Going somewhere?" I said.

"I have to go in for dialysis today," he said, nonchalantly. "And, oh yeah, the doctor called and they have a kidney waiting for me."

"*What?!*" I shrieked as I ran to him and slugged him as we laughed with excitement. Friends and loved ones descended on the hospital. Jordan was prepared, but the surgery did not take place for another thirty hours. The tragic donor's organs had to be harvested all at once, and not all of the recipients and their hospitals were ready as quickly as we were.

The surgery was delayed: two hours, two hours, two hours more. Finally, at ten p.m., Jordan was wheeled into surgery. We ate oranges and crumb cakes, worked puzzles, played Suduku and board games, removed nail polish and gave ourselves manicures.

When it began, it was another five long hours before the doctor emerged.

"Everything went perfect," he said. "The kidney pinked up immediately and is producing a ton of urine."

I let out a long breath of relief. For some reason, I'd worried about something the doctor had said didn't matter. It was a right kidney, but they'd placed it on the left side. Why? My rugged son thought he'd bump it less on that side. And apparently his body welcomed it.

After two days in the ICU he walked tentatively, like a hunched-over little old man. Although surgical patients ordinarily spend a much longer time in the hospital, Jordan was released two days later.

"Hospitals aren't healthy places," one doctor said. He gave Jordan strict instructions on the importance of the new antirejection medications—IgA nephropathy can attack transplanted organs—and the importance of monitoring and treating his high blood pressure and other conditions with prednisone and other drugs. Jordan had also developed recurrent acid reflux, and those pills were necessary too.

The doctors, the nurses and even the social worker repeated the same message to Jordan: take these pills, take care of yourself, or you'll go back on dialysis and need another kidney. Jordan needed to wear a mask around people because of his suppressed immune system. He nodded: yeah, yeah.

The next months were rocky. The IgA did indeed assault the new organ. A couple of months after the surgery a sac developed around the kidney that had to be surgically removed after prior attempts to drain it. A year later flu-like symptoms led to a diagnosis of a BK virus and a hospital stay. We did not realize how seriously ill Jordan had been with this until we learned that his physician, Dr. Bunchman, had been so concerned that he'd spent the night at the hospital several nights in a row to keep a close watch. And for good reason—the virus caused more scarring to the kidney and raised his creatine levels.

But God wasn't through with Jordan's life. After the virus scare he went on to have two uneventful, normal teenage years. Our local paper ran a story about his graduation from high school—an indication of how our community had come to see Jordan as "their" son, too.

Jordan found after a year of college that he didn't take to academic life. He worked at Graafschap Hardware Store and OK Tire Store before joining YWAM. After three months of discipleship training in Australia, he participated in the outreach portion of the program in Mexico.

YWAM is a unique concept. The organization takes kids right out of high school and breaks them down spiritually so that they can be filled with the Holy Spirit. Then, full of joy and good news, they go out and share what they have learned with others.

Jordan's stay in Mexico was a time of wonders. He loved being out on the streets talking to people, and he saw miracles of healing every day—both physical and spiritual. In fact, the acid reflux that had plagued him for so long, even before the transplant, was cured after his team members prayed for his healing.

It was with a spirit of celebration that we met him at the airport upon his return. We surprised him with funny hats and glasses and clothes—and he surprised us with his new beard. We all agreed that six months was far too long for us to be separated from one another.

He went back to working at OK tire store, and the next year he went on a spring break trip with a friend to Florida. Heat, not enough liquids, too much fun: a combination that led to the discovery of a buildup of blood and protein in his urine when he returned home. We all knew what that meant. His kidneys were in trouble. Again. Jordan went to the emergency room and before long was admitted to the hospital with full-blown kidney failure.

How could this happen? After all our hopes and answered prayers, why would his health go into reverse? I thought of all the sleepless nights, the endless dialysis, the surgery and the infections and the scares. Could we go through this again?

I was filled with questions, for the doctors, for God, for Jordan. The explanation came from Jordan himself: despite all the warnings, he had stopped taking his kidney medications. I was angry! And disillusioned because of what I saw as a lack of responsibility. And so was our entire family. I had cancelled my own spring break trip because of this latest crisis. His sister DeeDee was getting married in a couple of months. It looked as though Jordan would need a new kidney right away. How could his big sister be expected to undergo major surgery right before her wedding?

But we are family. We all knew she would—and should. But why would Jordan knowingly put her into such danger?

"Go easy on him," the doctor told us. "Let me talk to him before you get any more angry. I will see if I can find out why he did this."

When the doctor left, there was complete silence in the waiting room. None of us knew what to say. No one had told Jordan how disappointed we were, and yet he must have known from our facial expressions. We sat there looking at the floor, contemplating this failure. When the doctor returned, we learned the reason for Jordan's actions—or lack of action.

"Your son says that his team members prayed for his acid reflux while he was in Mexico, and he was able to stop taking medications for it," the doctor began. "And so he wanted the Lord to heal his transplanted kidney completely, too. So he stopped taking the anti-rejection medications."

We looked at one another in astonishment. But Jordan's faith made sense. The doctor continued. "I told him that God had blessed him with a kidney that He Himself had made and that the medicines are also a gift from God, to take care of that kidney. And he's agreed that he will keep taking the medicines."

To tell the truth, I was still disappointed and a little angry. But in the coming days, when we saw the severity of his condition, we softened.

"His kidney function's situation is very serious," doctors told us. "It's probably impossible to regain what he has lost."

And yet I remained peeved because I had given up a paid-for condo and a long-awaited vacation. I'm not proud to admit that. It took me several days to get over that.

The doctors pledged to do all they could to save Jordan's kidney—and they did, with extreme measures. Six times Jordan underwent a painful, expensive blood-cleaning procedure called plasmapheresis in which the blood is removed from the body, the elements of the blood separated and the plasma and antirejection proteins are removed, and then the rest of the blood is returned to the body.

My place is with my children when they are hurting. And so I slept on a pull-out bed and made floral arrangements for Deedee's wedding reception. Friends came and fed my family, cared for Dulci, and once again showed their love for our family. I learned again the lesson that God's promises don't become less true with more trouble—that difficulties don't dilute them. God showed us mercy and healed our son once again. I think that God must have a very special future for a young man He's rescued so many times.

It has now been three years since this "learning experience." Jordan takes his medications faithfully and does all he can to maintain a healthy kidney. He's got a lot to live for—he began dating a good friend, Erin, who became his wife and is now about to become a mother, and him a father.

One of the doctors noted that we must indeed have a much higher power than his, because medically Jordan's recovery was impossible—you can't fix a kidney that badly damaged.

"We do have a power like that," I told him. "And we have our church and our family and our friends praying for us."

He smiled. "Well, it worked, because only a miracle could have cured this kidney."

I smiled back. "Our Lord still performs miracles today."

Part Four

THE BEAT GOES ON

20

A Rhythm of Grace

Although I have told the story of my life from behind my own eyes, so to speak, the other personality—very much a silent partner—that permeates this story is, of course, my husband Ron.

Early on in our marriage, his health problems had turned our newlywed bliss upside down. You never expect to begin your wedded days taking care of your husband. Those words "for better or worse, for richer or poorer, in sickness and in health" trip right off the tongue when you're a princess in a white lace gown. They sound quite different when your prince is the one in a gown—a hospital gown.

I kept myself busy taking care of his nose-diving health. Outwardly I was cheerful and efficient. And yet privately I was devastated with the fear of an uncertain future, and with the prospect that I would lose my husband and be left all alone, a childless widow in a ramshackle house with a table saw in the living room.

When I met him, one of the things I loved about him was his spirituality. He'd attended the same church his

whole life, where he led the singing and participated in
many activities. When we were first married he was our
spiritual leader, taking charge of devotionals and family
prayer. He insisted on a foundation of Christ as the center of our lives, even when he could no longer take that
active role of leadership because of his health.

I had wanted a spiritual leader, but I had also dreamed
of someone who would dote on me, hand me money for
frivolous purchases, take me out to dinner, chauffer me
around. Someone who would put the gas in the car, man-
age the bills, manicure the yard, make all the decisions,
discipline our children and lead our family.

A husband to take care of me.

And that was never going to be.

From the beginning I was aware that my attitudes
would set the tone for what was coming. No one said life
was going to be easy, I reminded myself. "In this life you
will have trouble," Jesus stated clearly. So I hitched up my
work clothes and set to it.

We slid irresistibly into the roles of caregiver and patient. Ron has always been a relaxed personality—I've often said he is so "laid back" that he could fall over!—and
as he succumbed quite naturally to the demanding physical weakness I became the fighter, the pusher, the fixer.

I remember the flurry of activity and responsibility
I felt. But I was balanced by Ron's calmness. From the
beginning he would assure me, "Everything is going to be
all right." His resolution was rock hard. He never wavered
in his expectation that God would be with us. Even as illness after illness ravaged his body, as he lost his sense of
balance, as he developed double vision, as he struggled
with depth perception and fatigue and memory loss and
slowing mobility, he never backed down from his belief
that God is good, that God cared about and for us.

He would tell you that he appreciated the fact that
I pushed him to finish the house that has become so

important in our lives. He would say that I gave him purpose when illness had drained him of the "fight" that he once had. If I would criticize him for what I call his "*que será, será*" approach, I would remind myself that this is akin in its own way to one of the criticisms that could have been aimed at me through all our illnesses. I've wondered whether my faith in God has come across to others as perhaps too naive. In fact, doctors have more than once accused me of having faith that was unrealistic.

Believe me, there has been more than enough of the "real" to go around. The truth is that, during Ron's hard times with his health, in some ways he has been almost like another child in that not only his caregiving but all of the decision-making have fallen on me. Surgeries and procedures often came with urgency—no time to philosophize: just get it done. Then he would need someone to take him to doctors' appointments and therapy, someone to give him the love and attention he deserved, someone to step forward and take the steering wheel of our marriage.

But what a rhythm of grace God has given us. I was able to take care of Ron during his early illnesses. Then, when he and I were so severely injured in the accident that took the life of our son Joshua, friends and family rushed in to help us and our young children.

Later, although many friends and family helped with subsequent health crises, it was Ron who was able to stay home with the healthy children, allowing me to spend days and nights at the hospital for weeks at a time—for instance, when Jordan was initially diagnosed with IgA nephropathy. Coming full circle, as the children in our family grew they stepped up to help with the younger ones, and when necessary, even with their dad.

Ron's continual decline in health didn't keep him from doing what he could in this partnership of marriage.

For that I am grateful. And I am so glad we decided together to have the children with which God has blessed us.

I think of the people who expressed disapproval that we "kept having children." Was it because they thought Ron and I couldn't take care of them? They have more than abundantly filled the void that my unmet expectations of marriage had created. Was it because, as people said, Ron wouldn't live to see them grown? Our youngest is in high school. Dulci, it's true, will always be dependent on us. But she, too, has outlived everyone's predictions.

I've learned two things about health issues. One is not to try to diagnosis illness or predict outcomes from looking on the internet. That's a waste of time. And second, nobody, no matter what their medical credentials, can predict a lifespan. That's God's business.

About ten years ago we had weathered the fierce storms of Ron's brain tumor, losing a son in an accident and recuperation from serious injuries ourselves, adjusting to a profoundly disabled daughter, and surmounting the challenges of an organ transplant for our son. It seemed at that point as though perhaps our lives would settle into some sort of normalcy.

Then one day I noticed that Ron had a mole on his back that had changed color, from dark brown to a light tan.

"I don't like the way that looks," I told him. "Let's get your doctor to look at it."

At that time both Misty and DeeDee were already studying at Calvin College. Because they were old enough to understand the dangers of the situation it was very hard on them not to be living at home. They had been weaned on near-death experiences. They knew the drill: they had grown up with a permanent condition—at least one family member sick and/or in the hospital.

Two days after an in-office biopsy on Ron's skin, the tests came back. Cancer. More extensive biopsies and worse news: stage four cancer, in the lymph nodes. *"Really?"* I thought. "Cancer a third time? Really, God? What did we do? What do you want? How much more can we take?" I felt numb, as though I were drained, just going through the motions of life. Yet I somehow found the ability to communicate with God: "Please, God, give me the strength and the peace and patience to glorify Your name through this new journey."

But Ron already had that peace. "Don't worry, Von," he assured me. "Everything will be okay. God will take care of this as He always does." I shuddered. Maybe he was the one who wasn't being realistic. A stage four melanoma is serious. I knew people who had died with that diagnosis. But I didn't allow myself to think of what would happen if I lost Ron. At least I could take my stand on a middle ground. If I couldn't have the unbounded optimism Ron had, at least I could keep myself from thinking the worst.

Any positive view of the future was not shared by Ron's doctors. Radiation wouldn't help the melanoma, they said, and if we wanted to try chemotherapy we should know that it was successful in only about fifteen percent of cases.

"It will make Ron really sick," one doctor warned. "Chemotherapy is hard."

In addition, Ron would have to take interferon, a medication that can fight stage four cancer. I knew how difficult that would be, since I'd taken it for hepatitis, where it had served as an antiviral. Nonetheless Ron opted for chemotherapy. The night he was hospitalized to insert a port into his chest, our oldest child Misty was with us. She was having some severe back pains, so I went with her down to the emergency room, where a CT scan revealed that she had two kidney stones.

"Go figure," I told her. "When we are dealing with one thing, there's always one more . . . " But there were two more. Just as Ron began the chemotherapy, another of our daughters, Sadie, broke her arm. "Just another hurdle," I pronounced.

Unfortunately Ron could tolerate his chemotherapy for only about two or three months. "Everything tastes like iron," he complained. He stopped eating and drinking and began sleeping most of the time. His weight began a downward slide that ended with him being thinner than me—and that's pretty thin.

One day in the midst of this we were to have family portraits taken at church for a directory. It was no small task to get everyone dressed in matching clothing and out the door on time for our appointment. But when our turn came we couldn't find Ron. Some of the children found him alone in the hallway. He felt so dreadful that he was in tears. Our daughter Misty says that was one of only two times she'd ever seen her father cry.

When he was able we discussed whether or not he should continue with the chemotherapy. We began to pray that God would help us to know what to do. By the time Ron went to the doctor to discuss it, he was so weak that he staggered into the office. When he told his doctor he wanted to stop the chemotherapy, she was very negative.

"Okay, your decision," she said tersely. From that time on every time Ron came to her office for a checkup she seemed shocked that he was still alive.

Ron, not the doctor, was right in the end. He had said that God had helped us before and would help us now, and He did. We believed the decision to stop the chemotherapy was the correct one, and God gave us peace with our decision. We did not look back.

It took a while for some of Ron's strength to return, and this melanoma incident marked the end of his working days before he went on disability. Even on the doctor's portion of the disability application his doctor wrote that he would "not live long."

Was it Ron's nine lives? No, it was the blessings of God on our difficult circumstances: every blood test and scan in the decade that has passed since that time has been clear. The port in his chest (which the doctors told us would never be removed) did indeed come out. Although he's had other skin growths (both cancerous and precancerous) removed, his lymph nodes have stayed cancer-free.

21

THE HEAVIEST PRICES

It seems that everyone in our family has had a significant health issue. DeeDee was perfectly healthy until her senior year in high school. Our oldest, Misty, had gone on to college, and DeeDee was feeling the pressure of being the oldest child at home. She was involved with many extracurricular activities at school and trying to balance all that with what was going on in our lives, added to the death of Ron's father and Jordan's kidney crises. Uncharacteristically, she began to shy away from any public activities, saying she just wanted to stay home with me.

One day when we were out running errands, I looked at her and noticed she had a green tinge to her skin. I took her immediately to the emergency room, where they gave her two bags of fluids. Upon being questioned DeeDee admitted that she hadn't been eating and drinking for days. But that wasn't the underlying problem— something else was needed. She wouldn't open up to the specialist who examined her, and only after her pediatric doctor suggested and prescribed an antidepressive for depression and panic attacks did she begin to improve.

Once again I was the momma bear—when it's your daughter, you get to the bottom of the illness and get your child the treatment she needs.

When our Isabella became a senior in high school, she had panic attacks as well. This time we knew what course of action to take. Even now, though, Belle is dealing with stomach issues and fainting. We are trying to find out what's behind that.

Mercedes (Sadie) has dealt with migraine headaches since she was a little girl. They have become a familiar, though unwelcome, presence in her young life—she can now predict the onset of a migraine by the aura that precedes the terrible pain, nausea and sensitivity to light. She also was recently diagnosed with scoliosis or curvature of the spine, a hereditary condition that both Dulci and I also have. Sadie has physical therapy twice a week for pain management. Jordan had his kidney crises. Dulci will always be a child. And I recovered from an automobile accident and subsequent complications before battling hepatitis.

Without a doubt, though, Ron has paid the heaviest prices in this life: not only with his health but in terms of his ability to work and make a living for his family. Recently he had to give up yet another activity that means so much to men in general and to a car lover in particular.

He has been involved in numerous automobile accidents, the most recent of which, a year ago, was serious and his fault. He had forgotten to take his thyroid medicine and was so impaired that he wasn't alert enough to see a semi truck coming toward him.

"I've seen lots of wrecks at that intersection," the wrecker truck driver remarked about the site of the accident where five roads meet. "No one survives."

The semi's "Peterbilt" logo flew through the window and landed in Ron's front seat. All the glass was blasted out by the impact. Hearing aids, glasses, the GPS and the other contents of the little red truck—supplies that Ron had been transporting for our son-in-law's business— were scattered all over the snowy roadway. The other driver did survive, unhurt; and so did Ron, albeit with three broken ribs and some cuts.

Ron's driving days were over. I reproached myself—I knew the roads were slick: why didn't I tell him not to drive that day? Was I being too controlling in agreeing that he not drive anymore? Could a doctor perhaps provide some help?

The answer did not lie only in taking the medications as ordered. After an evaluation his doctor concluded that Ron's bodily response to all of his illnesses was that he was aging more rapidly than normal. And even when he takes his medicines there are other unpleasant and debilitating side effects. It's a vicious circle. It's being caught between a rock and a hard place. We both hate it.

Now, after a year of not driving, Ron is very content to stay at home. When he can he works in his wood shop, where he listens to Christian music at full blast and his favorite Christian comedians. Our home is filled with his wonderful creations. When he can't do that, as is the case much of the time, he just sleeps.

"Pain," he says soberly, "is not my friend."

He struggles with depression—understandable, considering his condition and his family history of depression. I confess that I don't understand depression. I am told that much of it is chemical. It is not something I've ever experienced personally, though. When he has bad days, we get through it. When he has good days, I wish every day were like that.

He has a hard time being around large groups of people because of his issues with balance, and his hearing makes communication difficult. He loves visiting with friends one-on-one in quiet places. We are blessed to enjoy such visits when others invite us to their homes.

He participates once a week in a small group Bible study with other men at our church library, some of whom are able to transport him. They are a close-knit group, something Ron needs and cherishes. Just this week a group of them came and unloaded wood for our heating stove. He is very blessed, and he knows it.

As his health declines, Ron is increasingly content to read his Bible devotionals and worship at home. Because of Dulci's vulnerability to illnesses, she doesn't go to church anymore either. On Sundays you'll find them in our home, surrounded by beautiful furniture Ron has crafted in a house he chose and resurrected, and the ever-present afterglow of the love of wife and sons and daughters, wherever they are.

22

MOUNTAINS OF MERCY

How profoundly our lives have changed, mine and Ron's, in thirty years. He used to be hot all the time and me cold, and now those roles have reversed. He can see close up, while I can see far away. He doesn't remember and I have to remind; he can't hear and I have to repeat. He lost his job. I work two. He can't be the husband he wanted to be; I have become both spouses and mourn his lost dignity. He sleeps all the time, and I live on four or five hours a night. I once ran to keep up with his long-legged stride and now I walk beside him, slowly, slowly. Once he was my protector; now I am his.

Did I make a mistake, early on, in taking so much off Ron's shoulders? Do I now? As Ron struggles with questions about his self-worth and with his physical pain, I glance over at his sleeping form. I am profoundly lonely, and it is an old, familiar feeling.

My children are growing up and one by one transferring their affections—as they should—to their spouses. Misty, now Mrs. Jordan Sligh, has her husband we refer to as "J2" to distinguish him in conversation from our son

Jordan. Maxwell, born in 2003, is J2's son and Misty and Jordan's little buddy. DeeDee is now Mrs. Derek DeFrell. And our Jordan is now married to his new wife, Erin, who will soon be delivering our first birth grandchild.

And yet, in their absence, I grieve. I work a second job as a caregiver for the elderly and fragile. I hold closely the sweetness that is Dulci, my eyes straying to now-empty cradles. My soul yearns for grandchildren. Daily I battle my own imperfection. I get frustrated. I am unkind. I get angry, yell, scream.

Was all this supposed to build patience? I'm sorry, but I have far less than I did years ago. And yet . . . And yet I know what God has said in James 1:2–4:

> Consider it pure joy, my brothers and sisters, whenever you face trials of many kinds, because you know that the testing of your faith produces perseverance. Let perseverance finish its work so that you may be mature and complete, not lacking anything.

After thirty years I'm far from mature. Still, though having been ground fine for decades between the millstones of many crises, I have learned some things in the process. I can't change people. I've tried. I can cooperate with God as He changes people, but that isn't my job. In particular, I can't change Ron. I pursue those things that only Ron and I can give each other: love and acceptance of each other, along with a daily struggle against disappointment and bitterness that are the tools of the devil, who would tear our home apart.

I've learned the difference between duty and rightness. Duty has its own rewards, and they are limited. But doing something because it is the right thing to do means that I take my place in a vast, eternal framework that God not only superintends but in which He becomes intimately involved. And if He Himself is the only reward, that is more than enough.

I have gone through the cycles of crisis. After the initial shock of an illness, a setback and a death, I have felt angry, cried out my questions to God, poured out my tears. I have asked, "Why my husband, and not somebody else's?"

"Why my child?"

"Why my *children*? All of them?"

But then God has given me the grace to step back from the situation and choose my attitude about it. I know I'm weak. I know that each situation we've faced has cost us physically, financially and emotionally. But when I am weak, there's a strength outside myself that I latch onto. I have lived 2 Corinthians 2:9–10:

> But he said to me, "My grace is sufficient for you, for my power is made perfect in weakness." Therefore I will boast all the more gladly about my weaknesses, so that Christ's power may rest on me. That is why, for Christ's sake, I delight in weaknesses, in insults, in hardships, in persecutions, in difficulties. For when I am weak, then I am strong.

I feel a new kind of weakness now, not one caused by crises. I rise stiff and sore each morning from bed. I reach for my bifocals and wonder why they are making the print in phone books so much smaller these days. I call my children by their siblings' names. I do what I swore I'd never do: sometimes I listen to the same music my parents did, and at other times I just ride in the car in silence.

People might ask me for the secret to living a life filled with trauma and uncertainty. I'm afraid I might disappoint them with my simplicity, but I must tell the truth: if I think I can change a bad situation for loved ones I'll fight ferociously and tirelessly for them. But if I can't change a situation I shift gears. I don't think about it. I just stay busy and do what I can to show my love to suffering people. I cope by serving. I accept what I have been given, and I move on. Other people may serve Him in different ways. But ministering to others is how I deny myself, take up my cross and follow Him.

Another rock-hard resource I have is my ongoing commitment to my own daily walk with the Lord. Deep, satisfying Bible study, heartfelt prayer, and quiet times of reflection are the cherished, sweet wells from which I daily draw my strength in "everyday" situations.

I also have the privilege of making a statement with my life by keeping my commitments to Ron. I understand how a marriage can be destroyed by chronic and repeated illnesses, by financial reverses, by the challenges of a special needs child, and most especially by the unbearable loss of a young son. But my commitments to my husband stand—and with God's help will always stand.

Where did my strength come from in these painful situations? I fell back on the Scriptures my parents had taught me, that I had learned in sweet fellowship studies with other Christians, along with the truths from gospel songs. They were there in my heart and my mind, ready when I needed them. In times of decision I hear my daddy's voice guiding me. It reminds me of Isaiah 30:20–21:

> Although the Lord gives you the bread of adversity and the water of affliction, your teachers will be hidden no more; with your own eyes you will see them. Whether you turn to the right or to the left, your ears will hear a voice behind you, saying, "This is the way; walk in it."

And that gift of a voice in their heads is one that my children know too. Jordan, especially, tells me that he hears *my* voice in his head sometimes when he is uncertain about what to do in a situation.

Ah, that's good, I say.

The circumstances of life my children have faced are not ones I would have chosen for them. I would never have said, yes, give us sickness and transplants and disability and bereavement. But there's a secret that carried me through when the medical prayers weren't answered, when the diagnosis did not bring hope, when a funeral loomed. The apostle Paul said he learned that secret—to be content no matter what the situation—and I have slowly and painfully learned it too.

Along the way our family has come to value joy far above happiness. Happiness is getting what you want. Joy is not about getting; it's about serving and giving. It brings with it the fruit of the Spirit.

If we have a "family Bible verse," it is Jeremiah 29:11— "'For I know the plans I have for you,' declares the LORD, 'plans to prosper you and not to harm you, plans to give you hope and a future.'"

You see, God had those plans for us all along. He always intended to give us a future. He always wanted us to have hope.

How hard has this been? Very, very hard. But look what we have! We have six faithful children who know how to weather storms. They love the Lord with all their hearts. Those who have married have Christian spouses.

Perhaps Ron says it best, when he looks with satisfaction at all our children: "Now this is what I call success."

We live with an angel. And we have one child who finished his tasks and was accepted into the loving arms of God after only five years of life. Isn't that what it's all about? Isn't it about, as a family, reaching a finish line, where Jesus is cheering us on to finish a race? Isn't it really all about having Him say, "Well done, my faithful servants; enter into My rest"?

Our story is that of what ordinary people do, in extraordinary situations. Our marriage began with a non-negotiable faith in God and a rundown house. We shoveled the goat crap and yanked down walls. We scraped the blistered siding and sanded it. We hauled away the hypodermic needles and the abandoned food. We burrowed into the walls and dragged out the trash of generations, rotting old newspapers with advertisements and stories nobody cared about anymore stuck between the studs.

We got horses. We bought a dog. We made a baby.

We dedicated the house to God, and it became a symbol of our coming lives.

Then God came in and demolished walls and ripped open shingles and shook its foundation until we stood leaning for balance against the great wind He brought across our lives, our marriage, our family.

He brought us more drug paraphernalia than we'd ever dreamed of.

He reached inside us and brought into the light old stories we didn't know we had and certainly didn't want to deal with.

We made more babies, and they were just as flawed as we were, only we didn't know it.

Look at us:

Three who struggle with hearing.

One with a borrowed organ.

One who sees life in seasons, through an aura of pain.

One with a nose broken for twenty-five years and a body patched and pinned together.

One unsteady and wracked with tumors, eaten away here and there.

Two ambushed by unreasoning fears.

Three with curved spines.

One unspeaking, with her mind in the suspended animation of an infant's thoughts.

And one sleeping beneath the sod.

We are a parade of broken people, for even all our best cures are only temporary. One day we'll join our Joshua, my father, Ron's parents, . . . all those who have gone on in faith before us. We'll see people from all the ages of earth who have lived hard lives and yet knew the secrets we know, that God pulls us from the floods of trial and sets us up on mountains of mercy.

One day, everything will be set right. Everyone will be healed.

And this, all this, will have been more than worth it.